# THE SPIRIT OF THE
# COUNTER-REFORMATION

THE LATE H. OUTRAM EVENNETT

# THE SPIRIT OF THE
# COUNTER-REFORMATION

*The Birkbeck Lectures in Ecclesiastical History
given in the University of Cambridge
in May 1951*

BY THE LATE

## H. OUTRAM EVENNETT

EDITED
WITH A POSTSCRIPT BY

## JOHN BOSSY

CAMBRIDGE
AT THE UNIVERSITY PRESS
1968

Published by the Syndics of the Cambridge University Press
Bentley House, P.O. Box 92, 200 Euston Road, London, N.W. 1
American Branch: 32 East 57th Street, New York, N.Y. 10022

Library of Congress Catalogue Card Number: 68-11282

Printed in Great Britain
at the University Printing House, Cambridge
(Brooke Crutchley, University Printer)

D5728/2

# CONTENTS

# FOREWORD

HENRY OUTRAM EVENNETT

1901–1964

The lectures that form the chapters of this book were delivered by Evennett as Birkbeck Lecturer in ecclesiastical history at Cambridge in May, 1951. The Birkbeck Lecturer is appointed yearly by Trinity College, but the passage of time and the distinction of many of the past lecturers have given the series a status equivalent to that of a university foundation. No obligation of publication is attached to the office, but Evennett had originally intended to prepare his script for printing. In the event, his college work and later his failing health stood in the way. Added to this, he was always diffident of his powers. In the last years of his life he had indeed said to his friends that he no longer hoped or wished to publish his script.

The lectures, however, had made a great impression upon his audience, and when, after his death, his script was examined, the text was seen to be surprisingly fair, and it was decided to consider publication. In part this was an act of piety towards a well-loved friend and colleague, but in perhaps greater measure it was due to a desire to preserve at least some small printed memorial of the research of more than twenty years on a topic unfamiliar to English scholars and readers. The study of the spiritual life of a country or an epoch is a fairly recent addition to the group of relatives and dependants surrounding the 'straight' political history of an age. It had scarcely achieved rights of citizenship before the appearance of Henri Bremond's brilliant exposition of French religious sentiment. Subsequently, however, many continental scholars took the subject up, and the massive *Dictionnaire de Spiritualité*, still far from complete after more than thirty years, is evidence of their influence. In no epoch does the spiritual life, with its practitioners and its expositors, bulk larger than in the first fifty years of the Catholic Reformation of the sixteenth century, but the subject has never been treated in all its amplitude, and in England in academic circles it has been ignored. Evennett indeed stood alone, and was himself never widely recognised as a master. For this reason, therefore, if for no other, any serious work of his deserved, indeed demanded, the benefit of publication.

Even so the difficulty of securing adequate annotation for his text seemed at first prohibitive, as his own notes and references were fragmentary. Fortunately it was possible to enlist the help of Dr John Bossy, who had worked under Evennett as a research student on the sixteenth century, and readers will be able to judge of the success with which he has accomplished a wearying and unspectacular task. He has added a final chapter, as Evennett himself had intended to do, and in this, the fruit of his own studies, he discusses the reasons for the relative or apparent failure of the Catholic Reformation to dominate the religious history of countries north of the Alps and the Pyrenees, with the exception of France.

For those unacquainted with the author, whom a distinguished Oxford medievalist once referred to as 'one of those unknown Cambridge historians', it may be in place to add a few words of introduction. Henry Outram Evennett was born in London in 1901. His father was a stockbroker; his mother, one of a large family, had a quota of Spanish blood and connections with South America. Evennett himself in later life wrote and spoke Spanish with ease, and the ancestral link had undoubtedly an influence upon his historical interests. His childhood was in some ways a lonely one, and his only constant companion, in a London house with no garden, was his sister. After their mother's death they shared a house, at first in London and later at Aspley Guise, near Bletchley, and this was his home during a large part of vacations in the later years of his life.

In due course he was sent to the school, then small and undistinguished, attached to the Benedictine priory at Ealing, but the headmaster, Dom Denis Goolden, had the insight and generosity to advise his mother to transfer him to Downside. The three years (1918–20) which he spent there changed the course of his life. He found mental and social stimulus, made friends for life among his schoolfellows, masters and the community, and owing in part to the encouragement of Dom Lucius Graham, his history master, succeeded in winning an exhibition at Trinity College, where, after two terms, he was elected into a senior scholarship. Trinity completed what Downside had begun in developing his talents and social gifts, and it remained his home, with brief interruptions, for more than forty years. Going up in 1920, he was a contemporary of Herbert Butterfield, Michael Oakeshott, and George Kitson Clark, the last named of whom became a lifelong friend. At first reserved and hesitant, he gradually widened his circle of friends, assisted by exceptional gifts as a pianist which he was willing to use on demand for any occasion grave or gay. He had indeed a genuine talent, which lent distinction to many May Week concerts, and for a time he seriously considered a musical career and appeared once or twice on public concert platforms, but Trinity and history won the day, happily for all concerned, and after two years he was elected to a Research Fellowship at Trinity in 1925, and to a teaching Fellowship in 1930. Thenceforth his residence was broken only by the war of 1939–45, for much of which he served with other academics in a government establishment at Bletchley, and by rare sabbatical absences. Returning to Trinity in 1945, he acted as one of the college tutors for ten years (1945–55). At Cambridge, in contrast to Oxford, the tutor as such has no teaching duties, but is responsible for all the relations between his pupils and the college and university. At Trinity each of the four tutors has heavy administrative and pastoral duties in connection with a large number of undergraduates, and Evennett was supremely successful in this work, using his gifts of humour, common sense and sympathetic understanding for the benefit of a long succession of pupils. Before the war, he had been a successful lecturer on political thought; in later years, lecturing on other subjects, he lost some of his ability to hold a class. Lecturing, like concert performance, always exacted a price of apprehension. Even after years of experience, he was always *incommunicado* from the end of Hall till his appearance at ten o'clock the next morning in the lecture-room. After some years of poor health, he was seriously ill in 1963, and in spite of a recovery died after a few days' illness on 1 October, 1964.

As an undergraduate reading for Part II of the History Tripos he had chosen as his Special Subject the course on the Council of Trent taught by R. Vere Laurence, and his subsequent research had issue in his only considerable book, a study of the Tridentine Cardinal of Lorraine. This remains an indispensable work of reference but it is tied, like many first-fruits of research, too rigidly to details and narrative. Nevertheless, a reader is often arrested by glimpses of an insight into the spiritual climate of the age, seen as a background. Throughout his career Evennett was occupied with an endeavour to master the vast literature of the Council of Trent, of which he hoped to write the definitive history. This was not to be, though in his last years he completed a few chapters. His own diffidence and lack of decision impeded him, and later the European war and his failing health. Moreover, while he delayed, a scholar with all the requisite qualities of industry and application had appeared in Germany in the person of Hubert Jedin, with whom he corresponded in friendly fashion over the years while Jedin was preparing for, and ultimately writing, the history of which Evennett had hoped to be the author.

In later years, indeed, his interest had turned from theological and political topics to those more directly spiritual. Devout from boyhood, he had felt for a time an attraction towards the monastic life, and although he decided otherwise, he never lost his love for Downside and his friends there, and his familiarity with the inside of a large religious house deepened his understanding of the aspirations and asperities of an earlier age. He was able, for example, to approach Jesuit history without showing himself either a partisan or a biased critic of the Society, and he was able to get behind the arid and often unedifying controversies to the real issues of spiritual warmth and depth. Many readers of his occasional pieces—a short pamphlet on the Reformation, a valuable chapter on the religious orders in the *New Cambridge*

## Foreword

*Modern History*, and a more recent broadcast talk on the Counter-Reformation—will have caught the undertones of a voice of a different timbre from that of any other English historian of the Reformation age. It is to preserve a fuller record of that voice that these lectures are published. They cannot fully present Outram Evennett's lovable personality to those who never knew him. His deep but altogether unassuming piety, his judgment of character, his ready sense of humour, and above all his readiness to give and to receive affection and his loyalty to all his friends won for him a unique place in the life of his College and Faculty, and will remain in the memories of those who knew him. But others also may be able to see in these pages something of the writer as a person as well as an historian.

DAVID KNOWLES

# EDITOR'S PREFACE

I have established the text of the lectures, which reproduces with minor adjustment the final state of Evennett's manuscript; replaced the original opening of chapter 1, of no great interest outside the room in which it was given, by the present first paragraph; written the Postscript, for reasons which I explain at the beginning of it; and added the footnotes. These are not meant to be exhaustive, but to provide details of works and passages cited in the text and a reasonable guide to the literature of the subject. I have kept further discussion for the Postscript, to which I refer when appropriate; and I do not claim to have read all the works cited elsewhere. I am also responsible for the title of the book and of some of its chapters.

I should like to express my thanks to all those to whom I owe the opportunity of undertaking so rewarding a task, especially Dr Kitson Clark; and also, for various kinds of help in carrying it out, to Professor Knowles, Dr G. R. Elton, and my brother Michael, of the Society of Jesus. None of them may be assumed to agree with anything I have written.

JOHN BOSSY

# TOWARDS A NEW DEFINITION

[In 1951, when Evennett gave these lectures, it had not yet become a commonplace to announce, amid general relief, that the Counter-Reformation was over. I doubt if, more than anyone else, he foresaw the events which have seemed to confirm the news of its passing; but I do not believe that they would greatly have changed his views. All that he wrote testified to his conviction that 'spiritual rebirth and enlightenment...are not achieved at ecumenical councils; they occur in solitude, or by contact with individuals who have themselves been spiritually reborn and enlightened'.[1] He came, certainly not to bury the Counter-Reformation, and not precisely to praise it, but to suggest that it, too, was a response to the conditions of its time, circumscribed, like others, by those conditions, but deep and creative enough to inspire modes of feeling and ideals of behaviour, a spirit, in short, which the Christianity of any time and place will be the worse for neglecting.]

Let me say at once that I have no startling discoveries to announce, hot-foot from the archive-room; nor, on so large a subject as I have chosen, could I harbour any illusive ambition of modifying accepted views. The subject of the Counter-Reformation is large; its definition and analysis difficult; its literature, scattered over many European languages, not always easy of access for a dweller in Cambridge. More and more, as I have striven in these last few years to acquaint myself adequately with the great mass of work produced in German, Spanish, Italian and French on the Counter-Reformation—not to mention more exotic languages—has there been borne in upon me an unhappy consciousness of amateur status, to the sapping of such small amount of self-confidence as I may once have felt in my ability to carry through the perhaps too ambitious programme that I originally formed for these lectures. But more and more, also, has the conviction

[1] Aelred Graham, 'The Pathos of Vatican II', *Encounter* (December, 1965), p. 17; compare Evennett's remarks in his broadcast talk, 'The Counter-Reformation', in J. Hurstfield (ed.), *The Reformation crisis* (London, 1965), p. 61. This talk was given in 1962.

grown that here is a field where important work is going on, the results of which have still to be adequately judged and assimilated in this country. Furthermore, I have come to ask myself afresh how we should best seek to study and understand this phenomenon which we call the Counter-Reformation, and how we should approach the task of assessing its meaning and its true significance in European, indeed in world, history. It is towards this task that these lectures are offered as a small and tentative contribution. Since the Counter-Reformation first gained a *droit de cité* among the recognised great movements in history, not only has our factual knowledge of it been greatly increased by the multiplication of sources, but our historical perspectives and our sense of values have been much altered by the passage of a hundred revolutionary years. We must not allow our freedom of historical thought to be constricted by the suggestions conveyed in a conventional label. The word 'Counter-Reformation', like the word 'Renaissance', combines the implication of much that is obviously true with much that is highly misleading. No doubt it now misleads us less badly than it would a historian descending —shall we say—from a flying saucer, because we know enough to discount the face value of conventional historical labels, and I for my part am as willing to agree to 'Counter-Reformation' as an accepted if conventional historical expression as I am to accept 'Reformation' or 'Renaissance'—or, for that matter, 'Evangelical'—on similar terms. Yet the word has had a certain constricting effect upon the evolution of historical thought about its subject-matter, and has perhaps contributed to a certain delay in modernising the historical treatment of the Catholic Church in the sixteenth and seventeenth centuries.

Other factors, admittedly, have contributed to this. Has there not been a certain tendency for post-medieval ecclesiastical history to become imprisoned within its own categories?—a certain shyness to seek appropriate illumination from the fact of the inevitable and organic connections of ecclesiastical bodies with the movements and forces of history in other spheres? Perhaps I exaggerate here; or perhaps the inevitable inter-relations and interdependencies between secular and ecclesiastical have been worked out only in some ways and not in others. Be this as it may, I feel convinced that in the case with which we are dealing, the concept of the Counter-Reformation as essentially 'reactionary' and backward-looking has tended to obscure, and certainly to obstruct, any attempt to synthesise the many ways in which it was, in effect, the evolutionary adaptation of the Catholic religion and of the Catholic Church to new forces both in the spiritual and in the material order. The concept of 'baroque' has only partial application here and does not cover enough ground to serve as a complete expression of the new correlation between Catholicism and the post-medieval world. On the other hand, and perhaps somewhat paradoxically, it would seem that there has been an insufficient liaison, so to speak, between the historians of the Church and the historians of religion—between the ecclesiastical historians proper and all those authors who in the last fifty years or so have done so much to explore, map and illuminate something that, for a Christian believer, is basic to the inner life of the Church, and should surely therefore be basic to Church history, namely, the history of spirituality—devotion, prayer, mysticism. In a still obscure way, I feel that in the combination of these two approaches, the better integration of the history of spirituality into ecclesiastical history on the one hand, and on the other the fuller recognition of the necessary organic similarities in the evolution of ecclesiastical and secular societies, there may lie the way to a new and perhaps more fruitful mode of ecclesiastical history—the two aspects representing a kind of mysterious body–soul relationship within the Church. At any rate, it is these two ideas which have mainly been in my mind in preparing these lectures. I am only too much conscious of all the imperfections and disproportions in the particular ways in which I have chosen to try to follow them out, and of how many well-worn themes in Counter-Reformation history—even that of the Council of Trent—will not, no doubt disappointingly, figure separately here. I have not tried to present a complete or final picture, only to make a few suggestions. It may be that if these lectures attain a published form some more coherent general view may emerge.

## The Spirit of the Counter-Reformation

I propose today to examine briefly the history of the concept of the Counter-Reformation.[1] When, in the period of the formation of the grand perspectives of European history by the nineteenth-century Romantics, the twin colossuses of 'Renaissance' and 'Reformation' stood out in linked greatness—the William and Mary, so to speak, of liberated, progressive post-medieval Europe—the fate of Catholicism seemed of secondary interest only. Nor could the revival of Catholicism after the end of the Napoleonic period offset the conviction of many intellectuals, a conviction later strengthened by the events of Pius IX's pontificate, that the Catholic Church, then as earlier, was doomed, rightly and inevitably, to be on the losing side in the struggle for progress; that, though perhaps something more than a mere persistent survival, she had no claim to be reckoned among the forces—let alone the salutary forces—that had a positive part to play in the making of the future of mankind. The reform of Catholicism in the sixteenth century and its struggle against the 'progressive' forces of Renaissance and Reformation could only be peripheral to the really significant, creative, movements of that age, and could only be worthy of study in that light. Even Catholic historical scholarship, chartless and rudderless for the most part in this respect, hardly sought to synthesise but was content to record, piecemeal, reforms, resistances, counter-offensives. Nor was the evolutionary idea invoked—perhaps understandably—as an aid towards the interpretation of former stages and vicissitudes in the Church's history.

The German word *Gegenreformation*, which has been borrowed by and translated into other languages, did not, when first employed, signify a single large-scale historical movement. It seems to have made its appearance towards the end of the eighteenth century for the purpose of describing any local reversal of the Reformation, any particular instance, for example in Germany, of the regaining of a territory formerly Protestant, or of the extermination of Protestantism within a certain area.

[1] Cf. A. Elkan, 'Entstehung und Entwicklung des Begriffes Gegenreformation', *Historische Zeitschrift*, CXII (1924), 473–93, and Jedin's essay, *Katholische Reformation oder Gegenreformation?* (see p. 8).

It was thus susceptible of the plural number. The word, we are told, is not to be found in early nineteenth-century German dictionaries. But after the Napoleonic age growing familiarity with the concept of Counter-'Revolution' may well, it has been suggested, have made the general concept of Counter-'Reformation' more easily entertainable. A Counter-Reformation in the original episodical sense had most spectacularly occurred in Bohemia and in 1844 there appeared in Germany Pescheck's *Geschichte der Gegenreformation in Böhmen.*[1] But the larger potentialities lurking behind the word were first clearly seen by the perspicacious mind of Ranke. In his *Geschichte der Päpste,* the first volume of which was published in 1834,[2] Ranke in effect arrived at the concept of an important general movement of Catholic reform and resistance to Protestantism, in which such phenomena as the pontificates of the later sixteenth-century Popes, the story of the Jesuits and of the Council of Trent, hitherto treated episodically and in an isolated fashion, were brought within a grand synthesis. But in spite of his English translator, he still spoke of 'Counter Reformations' and not of 'The Counter Reformation'[3] and in 1843 he closed his history of Germany in the age of the Reformation with the words 'Auf das Zeitalter der Reformation folgte das der Gegenreformationen'.[4] In spite of the plural, however, it was a great deal that the 'idea' of Counter-Reformation had been introduced into the terminology of historical periodisation. Ranke, indeed, arrived at his general concept of a German if not a European period in which 'Counter-Reformation' was the dominant perceptible force, through his

[1] C. A. Pescheck, *Geschichte der Gegenreformation in Böhmen* (2 vols., Dresden/ Leipzig, 1844); the title of the English translation (London, 1845) is 'The Reformation and Anti-Reformation in Bohemia'.

[2] Originally published as vols. 2–4 of *Fürsten und Völker von Süd-Europa im sechszehnten und siebzehnten Jahrhundert* (4 vols., Berlin, earliest British Museum ed.1836–8); English translation by G. R. Dennis (3 vols., London, 1908).

[3] *Fürsten und Völker,* III, gives titles to fifth and seventh books as 'Gegenreformationen. Erster Zeitraum, 1563–89' and 'Zweiter Zeitraum, 1590–1630'; likewise other titles, pp. 36, 111. But, p. 399, 'Gegenreformation in Deutschland'. The English translation has 'Counter-Reformation' for all these.

[4] *Deutsche Geschichte im Zeitalter der Reformation* (5 vols., Berlin, earliest British Museum ed. 1839–52), v, 391. The words quoted are in fact at the end of the last paragraph but four. Cf. Elkan, *Historische Zeitschrift,* CXII, 486, who reads, however, 'Gegenreformation'.

studies on the papacy, and through the gradual formation in his mind of the picture of a morally and institutionally reinvigorated ecclesiastical institution taking into its hands the supreme direction of a widespread religious movement with important political aspects and implications. Naturally, Ranke had less interest in the purely religious side of this revived Catholicism than in its political consequences and manifestations. All the more so is it remarkable that it should have been this matter-of-fact Saxon, with all his inbred anti-Roman prejudices and his view that the papacy had no contemporary significance, who first grasped—almost willy-nilly—a complete picture of the Counter-Reformation as a whole. And let us not forget Macaulay's generous recognition in his famous essay on Ranke's 'Popes'.[1] After this no one could doubt that the Counter-Reformation had existence— a position in history, even though its magnitude might be disputed.

From about 1860 the Counter-Reformation as an important historical phenomenon of European significance became accepted by scholars both inside and outside Germany, though in 1852 the great F. C. Baur in his *Epochs of Church History*[2] had recognised neither the name nor the thing. But in 1866 Ritter lectured in Bonn on *Deutsche Geschichte im Zeitalter der Gegenreformation*[3] and then in 1880 Maurenbrecher, a pupil of von Sybel, published his important *Geschichte der katholischen Reformation*.[4] The new expression 'Catholic Reformation', though in truth it harked back to the eighteenth century and had never since been entirely discarded, was now deliberately reintroduced by Maurenbrecher, and his doing so constitutes a landmark in the development of this story. Ranke, for all his appreciation of the papal and Catholic achievement of the later sixteenth century, saw the whole movement as essentially a reflex defensive action which

---

[1] T. B. Macaulay, *Critical and historical essays* (Everyman's Library ed., 2 vols., London/New York, 1907), II, 38–72.

[2] F. C. Baur, *Die Epochen der kirchlichen Geschichtsschreibung* (Tübingen, 1852).

[3] M. Ritter, *Deutsche Geschichte im Zeitalter der Gegenreformation und des dreissigjährigen Krieges* (3 vols., Stuttgart, 1889–1908); according to Jedin, in his *Katholische Reformation oder Gegenreformation?*, mentioned on p. 8, the date was 1876.

[4] W. Maurenbrecher, *Geschichte der katholischen Reformation* (vol. 1 only published, Nordlingen, 1880); cf. Jedin, *Katholische Reformation oder Gegenreformation?*, pp. 11–12.

would not have come into being at all but for the challenge of Protestantism. Maurenbrecher came in the course of his studies to perceive that the 'Counter-Reformation' possessed roots striking down into pre-Reformation soil, and recognised that herein lay new and complicating problems for historians. The significance of this—especially as coming from a non-Catholic scholar—was not lost upon Catholic reviewers in Germany.

The question now raised was indeed crucial to the analysis and understanding of the group of phenomena hitherto labelled 'Counter-Reformation', but it had even greater significance. It opened up the way towards a new conception of two different, contemporaneous, and ultimately self-subsistent modes of religious and ecclesiastical reform arising out of the aspirations and confusions and uncertainties of the early sixteenth century— Protestantism and reformed Catholicism—in place of the simple earlier picture of mere Protestant action and Catholic reaction. This, surely, was of immeasurable importance in the general appreciation of European history as a whole. Jealous for their monopoly both of the word and of the concept 'Reformation', many Protestant scholars were quick to question the validity of Maurenbrecher's expression 'Catholic Reformation'; and soon a third competitor was introduced in the phrase 'Catholic Restoration'. This suited the prepossessions of those who refused to admit that any amount of internal reforming within the dogmatic and institutional framework handed down by the medi-eval Church could constitute a true Reformation with a capital 'R'. So deeply had the implications of the age-old conventional use of the word, Reformation, sunk into the subconscious mind of all scholars that it was not until von Pastor began to give currency to the phrase 'Catholic Reformation' that it acquired a wider usage. From his volume on Paul III, published in 1909, up to the volume, published in 1927, taking his narrative up to the death of Paul V in 1621, Pastor sub-titled his work *Geschichte der Päpste im Zeitalter der katholischen Reformation und Restauration*. From 1621 onwards up to 1644 the sub-title is *Geschichte der Päpste im Zeitalter der katholischen Restauration und des dreissigjährigen Krieges*. Nevertheless, it seems that

Pastor saw a point of real transition from Reformation to Restoration in the pontificate of Gregory XIII—the true aggressive element of 'counter' in the 'Counter-Reformation' thus emerging fully under Sixtus V and his successors.[1]

Simplified periodisings of this sort are apt, however, to be misleading, and though Pastor's work was monumental, in some ways outstanding, and certainly indispensable, it was weakest on its reflective, interpretative side. But the realisation that the Counter-Reformation, so called, contained within itself the element of independent, 'counterpart' internal reformation (as it were), in addition to its defensive-aggressive aspect, added extra complication to the study of its nature in action, as well as to the problem of its origins. In a learned and stimulating little book published in 1946, and entitled *Katholische Reformation oder Gegenreformation? Ein Versuch zur Klärung der Begriffe*,[2] Professor Hubert Jedin, now of Bonn, the greatest living authority on the Counter-Reformation, discussed very fully the different usages and meanings of the expressions 'Counter-Reformation', 'Catholic Reformation', 'Catholic Restoration' as variously employed over the last century or so.[3] He might also have added the expression 'contre-révolution religieuse' employed, uniquely, I think, by Philippson in his well-known work.[4] In so far as it helps us to clear our own minds as to how we can most usefully think about the phenomena under consideration, such a discussion is profitable, and all students of the sixteenth century should be in debt to Professor Jedin's unique little book; but it can hardly be doubted that scholars in all countries tend to use the conventional terms they are accustomed to, without necessarily committing themselves to the acceptance of a purely literal interpretation of them. Thus in Italy and Spain, for example, *Controriforma* and *Contrareforma* are conventionally used, as Counter-Reformation is in England, by writers who nonetheless

---

[1] L. von Pastor, *Geschichte der Päpste seit dem Ausgang des Mittelalters bis zum Tode Pius' VI* (Freiburg-im-B., 1889–; 2nd ed., 16 vols., 1901–): English translation (40 vols., London, 1891–1953): see XIX, 2; cf. Jedin, *Katholische Reformation oder Gegenreformation?*, pp. 16 ff.

[2] Luzern, 1946.       [3] *Ibid.* pp. 25–38.

[4] M. Philippson, *Les origines du catholicisme moderne: la contre-révolution religieuse au xvi<sup>e</sup> siècle* (Brussels, 1884).

accept the idea of an independent Catholic Reformation. In the hands of authors less firmly established in realities than Professor Jedin, too elaborate a discussion of terms and their usages might easily degenerate into pure logomachy. The combination and interaction of different purposes and different pressures within what I propose still to call the Counter-Reformation are too general and too subtle to be patient of an anatomical dissection which would lay out the specimens on three separate tables labelled Catholic Reform, Counter-Reformation and Catholic Restoration respectively. Such an operation would surely tend towards making nonsense of the real unity of history.

The difficulties of analysis and interpretation consequent upon the realisation of the double character, as it were, of the Counter-Reformation movement in action, appear also, though in a different way, when we consider the problem of origins. If, as I am inclined to think, the Reformation on its religious side and the Counter-Reformation on *its* religious side can reasonably be regarded as two different outcomes of the general aspiration towards religious regeneration which pervaded late fifteenth- and early sixteenth-century Europe, then the whole problem of tracking down each to its own sources, the problem, indeed, whether an absolutely clear-cut, mutually exclusive division of such sources is entertainable, immediately faces us. Both movements, to take one example only, have reasonably claimed some descent from the *devotio moderna*, that movement of northern piety—reflecting the rich Flemish and Netherlands civilisation—the influence of which was so pervasive and widespread. It is perhaps easier to detect here the 'precursors' of the Counter-Reformation—a conservative movement not destructive of old frameworks in spirituality, thought or institutions—than the 'precursors' of Protestantism, which came to a head in a whole revolution of religious psychology and religious values, finding its focal theological point in the doctrine of Justification by Faith alone and the view of Justification as more imputed than achieved. The ingenious attempts made by A. V. Müller, an ex-Dominican who questioned Denifle's knowledge and understanding of early medieval texts, to trace a *catena* of medieval teachers, mainly in Luther's own order of Augustinian friars, holding something very close to Lutheranism[1] have, on the whole, won acceptance neither by Catholic nor by Lutheran historians of theology. Yet, though it may be true that there was no special Augustinian tradition among the Augustinians, great interest nonetheless attaches to the theological views of the Augustinian friars in the sixteenth century as seen most notably in the life and works of Giles of Viterbo and of Girolamo Seripando, the latter so fully studied by Professor Jedin in a superb biography.[2]

What, however, were, in fact, the historical phenomena that convinced Maurenbrecher, and others after him, that the reforming elements in the Counter-Reformation did not take their rise wholly out of the fight against Protestantism but went back to earlier springs? The realisation of the existence of such earlier springs was—I would suggest—one of the indirect fruits of the advance in medieval studies that was contemporaneously producing, in the works of a variety of scholars, the attempt to push back the origins of the Renaissance itself to medieval—and in particular Franciscan—sources, and which, in general, was blurring the hitherto clear-cut line between 'Medieval' and 'Renaissance'. Ranke, concentrating his attention on the Popes of the sixteenth century and later, was not particularly concerned with the possible remoter spiritual influences behind the lives of Cajetan, Carafa, Giberti, Contarini and the rest, in whom, nonetheless, he recognised a true spiritual force which was ultimately unified and deployed for action by the papacy. Ranke touched the Spanish sources significantly only when he dealt with the utilisation by papacy and curia of St Ignatius and the Society of Jesus; and here, still focusing his judgments from the angle—as it were—of remote Wittenberg, he tended to see the great Basque saint and his followers simply as incarnating in

[1] A. V. Müller, *Luthers theologische Quellen: seine Verteidigung gegen Denifle und Grisar* (Giessen, 1912).
[2] H. Jedin, *Girolamo Seripando: sein Leben und Denken im Geisteskampf des 16. Jahrhunderts* (2 vols., Würzburg, 1937): English translation, omitting studies in vol. II, F. C. Eckhoff, *Papal legate at the Council of Trent: Cardinal Seripando* (St Louis/London, 1947).

religious garb the somewhat reactionary, though picturesque, knight-errantry of medieval Spanish chivalry—by itself a very inadequate analysis. Ranke never visited Simancas or the Escorial. Nor did he give serious attention to the life and institutions of the Spanish Church under Ferdinand and Isabella.

It was precisely this, the revivals and reforms in the Spanish Church dating from before the birth of Luther, and associated primarily with the name of Cardinal Jiménez de Cisneros,[1] that convinced Maurenbrecher not only that the Catholic reform had started in earnest before the Lutheran revolt, but that the Counter-Reformation in all its aspects was basically of Spanish inspiration. Researching on Philip II and Charles V at Simancas and Madrid as early as 1862, Maurenbrecher had found himself forced back to the study of the reign of Ferdinand and Isabella, as a result of which he came to his conclusion that the Catholic revival originated in Spain, that Spain inspired its first leaders in Italy— Adrian VI, Carafa, Contarini—, that Spanish theologians dominated at Trent, that the Spanish mystics placed an indelible mark upon Catholic spirituality, and that the Spanish-founded Society of Jesus impressed the marks of Spanish religious mentality—spirit and methods alike—on the whole counter-reformation Church. This Spanish mentality he himself regarded as archaic, reactionary, infertile, anti-German. Maurenbrecher, for all his services to the history of the Counter-Reformation, was not in any personal sympathy with it. He was a true German nationalist of his age, a supporter of Bismarck in the Kulturkampf; and after the publication of his book in 1880 he turned his professional attention to modern times and the study of the new German Empire. He had, however, established a thesis which was destined to endure, and which, while acceptable to Catholics because it upheld the independent origin of the Catholic reform of the sixteenth century, also gratified Teutonic Protestantism by stressing the reactionary, Latin, essentially non-Germanic nature of that origin. The thesis was re-stated by Eberhard

---

[1] See M. Bataillon, *Erasme et l'Espagne* (Paris, 1937), pp. 1–75; R. Aubenas and R. Ricard, *L'Eglise et la Renaissance, 1449–1517*, in A. Fliche and V. Martin, *Histoire de l'Eglise depuis les origines jusqu'à nos jours*, XV (s.l., 1951), 299–311.

## The Spirit of the Counter-Reformation

Gothein in his weighty volume *Ignatius von Loyola und die Gegenreformation*.[1] Though more alive than Maurenbrecher to the strength of purely Italian influences, Gothein nonetheless depicted the Counter-Reformation as a movement born in Spain, remaining always essentially Spanish, and, largely through the Jesuits, eventually hispanising the whole of modern Catholicism —in Italy, France, Germany and elsewhere—even when it was eventually brought under the control of that Italian institution, the papacy. Italy, France and Germany were—in his view—by and large, passive receivers of a Spanish article. Unlike Maurenbrecher, Gothein had never been to Spain to work at Spanish sources there. But he shared Maurenbrecher's anti-Spanish feelings. The same can be said, I think, of other German writers who accepted and propagated the Maurenbrecher–Gothein thesis, including Paul Herre, who investigated the papal conclaves of the sixteenth century.[2]

It is worth emphasising that this 'Spanish thesis' concerning the nature of the Catholic Reformation was built up by German Protestant historians most of whom had never been to Spain. Yet German Catholic scholars had not wholly neglected Spanish history. Döllinger had concerned himself with it, and had published documents; Hefele wrote a biography of Cardinal Jiménez de Cisneros.[3] But it is now recognised that the 'Spanish thesis' cannot be maintained to the full. Much more research is necessary before we can hope to get a reasonably full or secure picture of the Spanish Church and Spanish religion in the age of Ferdinand and Isabella or fully understand the nature and extent of original Spanish influence in the Counter-Reformation as a whole. Indeed, as I shall have occasion to suggest at more than one point later on, the Spanish influences themselves must be pushed back to what lies behind *them*, and in this process some of the important lines tend to run back from Iberia to

[1] Halle, 1895.
[2] *Papsttum und Papstwahl im Zeitalter Philipps II* (Leipzig, 1907).
[3] J. J. I. von Döllinger, *Beiträge zur politischen, kirchlichen und Cultur-Geschichte der sechs letzten Jahrhunderte* (3 vols., Regensburg/Vienna, 1862–82); C. J. von Hefele, *Der Cardinal Ximenes und die kirchlichen Zustände Spaniens am Ende des 15. und Anfange des 16. Jhdts* (Tübingen, 1844): English translation (London, 1860).

Italy, and to the Netherlands, and perhaps even to Germany. Spain, however, is still a country where, in spite of the laborious efforts of many archivists and scholars, prodigious masses of paper must still lie unexplored in numerous institutions, lay and ecclesiastical, and the consequent difficulties confronting systematic original research have affected all aspects of Spanish history, political and economic as well as religious.

There were, however, from an early time, those who believed that in the general acceptance of the 'Spanish thesis', the purely Italian, and other, sources of the early Counter-Reformation were in danger of being overlooked. This was felt by Franz Dittrich when he was preparing his biography of Contarini.[1] A new line had been opened up as early as 1859 in an article entitled *Die kirchliche Reform in Italien unmittelbar vor dem Tridentinum* by a Swabian priest, Joseph Kerker;[2] while the works of Constantin von Höfler suggested the notion of the Counter-Reformation as the true Romanic 'Reformation'.[3] Dittrich himself pursued the study of the fifteenth-century monastic reforms in Italy, and of the work of Giberti of Verona, in articles published in 1884.[4] During the last fifty years, the histories of the Roman Oratory of Divine Love; of the many other similar Italian oratories and pious associations; of the origins of the Theatines, and other Italian congregations, including the Oratorians, have all been much elucidated by Bianconi, Premoli, Padre Tacchi-Venturi, S. J., Monsignor Pio Paschini and others.[5] The obvious

---

[1] *Gasparo Contarini, 1483–1542* (Braunsberg, 1885).

[2] *Tübinger theologische Quartalschrift*, XLI (1859), 3–56.

[3] C. A. C. von Höfler, *Die romanische Welt und ihr Verhältnis zu den Reformideen des Mittelalters*, in Sitzungsberichte der Wiener Akademie, phil.-hist. Klasse, XCI (1878), 257–538, esp. 460 ff.

[4] F. Dittrich, 'Beiträge zur Geschichte der katholischen Reformation im ersten Drittel des 16. Jhdts', *Historisches Jahrbuch* (Görresgesellschaft), V (1884), 319–98; VII (1886), 1–50.

[5] A. Bianconi, *L'opera delle Compagnie del Divino Amore nella riforma cattolica* (Citta di Castello, 1914); O. M. Premoli, *Storia dei Barnabiti* (3 vols., Rome, 1913–25), and below, p. 27; P. Tacchi-Venturi, *Storia della Compagnia di Gesù in Italia* (Rome, 1910–), vol. I: *La vita religiosa in Italia durante la prima età della Compagnia di Gesù*; P. Paschini, *La beneficenza in Italia e le Compagnie del Divino Amore nei primi decenni del Cinquecento* (Rome, 1925), repr. in *Tre ricerche sulla storia della Chiesa nel Cinquecento* (Rome, 1945); also *S. Gaetano da Thiene, G. P. Carafa e le origini dei chierici regolari Teatini* (Rome, 1926).

fact of the purely Italian origin of the important Capuchin Franciscan reform, second only to the Society of Jesus in the final range and success of its counter-reformation apostolate, does not seem to have been much commented on in this context, but it is an outstanding proof of the continuation of the true Franciscan impulse in Italy.[1] But most of these Italian developments were post-1517 in origin, and so capable of construction—though perhaps wrongly so—as *Counter*-Reformation, rather than independent Catholic reform. It was primarily the massive work of von Pastor which swung the centre of gravity of Catholic reform and counter-reformation studies back from Spain to Italy.

Pastor, an Austrian by nationality, enormously widened the range and scope of counter-reformation studies, and gave a powerful impetus towards further research. He was a master of three essential things. First, he knew thoroughly the background of the German world and the Protestant Reformation. In this field he had been much influenced by Döllinger's studies and even more so by those of his own master and friend, Janssen, whose book,[2] for all its defects of presentation and its tendencies towards superficiality (characteristics, indeed, not wholly undetectable in Pastor too) had seriously ruffled the somewhat complacent waters of German Protestant historical scholarship, soon to be further disturbed by Denifle.[3] In the second place, Pastor was also a master of the Italian Renaissance, its politics and its culture, and although it can be held against him that his artistic interests made him too much prone to form his general ideas with reference to art concepts, his emphatic association of both pre- and post-Reformation Catholicism with the Renaissance on its cultural side helped to suggest the idea of internal spiritual forces developing uninterruptedly through the Catholicism of the

---

[1] Cf. Evennett, 'The New Orders', in G. R. Elton (ed.), *The New Cambridge Modern History*, II (Cambridge, 1958), ch. ix.

[2] J. Janssen, *Geschichte des deutschen Volkes seit dem Ausgang des Mittelalters* (8 vols., Freiburg-im-B., 1878–94; latest ed., 3 vols., Freiburg, 1913–17): English translation (17 vols., London, 1896–1925).

[3] H. S. Denifle, *Luther und Luthertum in der ersten Entwickelung* (2 vols., Mainz, 1903–9); *Ergänzungen* (2 vols., Mainz, 1905–6). For criticism and reception of Denifle, see Gordon Rupp, *The righteousness of God* (London, 1953), pp. 22 ff.

fifteenth and sixteenth centuries. Thirdly, either in person or through his many helpers, Pastor had explored and combed Italian archives with a thoroughness which had been entirely impossible in Ranke's time. As his work went ahead, he profited by the exploitation of the opening of the Vatican Archives by Leo XIII and the work done in them by German, Austrian and Italian scholars and societies: the labours of Hergenröther, Denifle, Ehrle, Mercati,[1] the Tridentine documents published by the *Görresgesellschaft*,[2] the great series of *Nuntiaturberichte aus Deutschland*[3] and much else. Like Ranke, however, Pastor was writing the history of the Popes, and not of the Counter-Reformation as such, and therefore while he had to take all Europe, to go no further afield, for his province, it was Europe as seen from the Roman centre, and the Roman and Italian influences naturally held the middle of the stage. Because his story went back into the fourteenth century, and because his large-scale picture of papal development represented the whole process as, in the last analysis, a spiritual and religious thing, the notion of the Counter-Reformation as a movement spreading outwards from Italy and first generated there through the action of deeply rooted forces, was easy to receive.

Philosophising about history, however, was not really Pastor's *métier*. His early attempt to distinguish between a Christian and a pagan Renaissance[4] produced too simplified a dichotomy and I do not know that he anywhere attempted a serious analysis of either the exact nature or the true historical significance of his subject-matter—the history of the Popes from the end of the Schism to the French Revolution, though perhaps his choice of terminals may have had significance. But the history of the Popes in the sixteenth and seventeenth centuries was so much bound up with the whole Counter-Reformation, even if, when used as a focal point, it necessarily overemphasised some aspects

---

[1] All officials of the Vatican Library or Archives: see *Enciclopedia cattolica*, under names.
[2] *Concilium Tridentinum. Diariorum, actorum, epistularum, tractatuum nova collectio* (Freiburg-im-B., 1901– : in progress).
[3] Published by Prussian (German) Historical Institute in Rome, Gotha, 1892– ; Austrian Cultural Institute in Rome, etc., Vienna, 1897– .
[4] *History of the Popes*, introductions to vols. I and V, esp. I, 13, and V, 97 f.

and tended to neglect others, that Pastor was often assumed to be writing specifically on the larger, more universal theme. Spanish critics of Pastor who stress the weakness of the Spanish side of his work appear to make this assumption. But there is some substance in the contention that Spanish affairs were the Achilles heel of the great Austrian master. No more than Ranke had he fully studied the Catholic revival under Ferdinand and Isabella—when Rome was at its maximum of secularisation—and nowhere in his work did he really fulfil his promise of going fully into the purely religious side of Spanish counter-reformation Catholicism from Cisneros to the Carmelites and Luis de León.[1] Thus, it is claimed by Spaniards that Pastor's severe treatment of Philip II and indeed his whole attitude toward Hispano-papal relations in the sixteenth century is dominated by political considerations and that he appears unmoved and uninfluenced by the vivid, gripping story of Spanish spirituality in this age.[2] About Italy and her beauties, Pastor, true German that he was, felt with deep romantic emotion. Spain he never visited. His eyes never saw the walls of Ávila, or the view from them of the burning Castilian plain; he never gazed upon the majesties of Compostela, or the richness of Salamanca or the weird peaks of Montserrat...

The general tendency of Pastor's work, therefore, was to redress, and perhaps to over-redress, the balance that Maurenbrecher, Gothein and others had swung so heavily in favour of Spain as the real begetter and imposer of the Counter-Reformation on Europe. Recent work, however, has brought out clearly the strength of native Italian sources in the religious revival. The influence and multiplicity of the many semi-lay, semi-ecclesiastical associations of the type of the Oratories of Divine Love have come in fuller light—and the influence of the Roman oratory by itself has been seen to have been exaggerated. The development

---

[1] I cannot find a promise to this effect in the *History of the Popes*; some remarks in x, 388.

[2] P. Leturia, 'Pastor, España y la restauración católica', *Razon y Fe*, LXXXV (1928), 136–55. I have only seen Evennett's notes on this article, which seems comparable in importance for the historiography of the Counter-Reformation to the essays of Elkan and Jedin cited above, pp. 4 n., 8.

of the whole pregnant spiritual climate in so many of the Italian cities—Venice, Milan, Brescia, Florence, Naples—out of which sprang the first Italian congregations of reformed priests, Theatines, Barnabites, Somaschi, Oratorians, and also the foundations of St Angela, has been much explored. The powerful yet hidden influence of so many remarkable women in the Italian contemplative convents has been revealed; a new realisation exists of the great intellectual stature of Cajetan de Vio,[1] despite the weakness of his dealings with Luther. In addition, the close links between Italy and Spain suggest many traces of an intercourse that operated on the spiritual as well as the secular plane: links between the north Italian and the Castilian Dominicans; more precisely the wide influence of Savonarola, undoubtedly powerful in the religious, less so perhaps in the intellectual, development of the Preachers in Castille.[2] Let me quote here—in translation—some words of Marcel Bataillon taken from a study of Italian influences on Spanish spirituality entitled *De Savonarole à Louis de Grenade:*

Here we catch a glimpse of a little-explored zone of spiritual links between the two countries which, it is said, created the Counter-Reformation. A zone all the more obscure in that the Inquisition has thrown heavy shadows upon it by prohibiting certain books and bringing their authors under suspicion [here the reference is chiefly to the Italian Dominican Fra Battista da Crema]. It seems, however, that here we are at the very heart of the movement which the term Counter-Reformation expresses so badly. Its apostles are engaged in very nearly the same combat as Savonarola and the *piagnoni* half a century earlier, and they are engaged on it with so little thought of the Protestant menace that they end by incurring the suspicion of Lutheranism.[3]

The influence of Spanish religious writers in Italy—Valdés, for example, and St Ignatius—is well known. The reverse influence far less so. I quote M. Bataillon again:

[1] See bibliography, especially extensive after 1934, in *Enciclopedia cattolica*, IV, 1506–10.
[2] V. Beltrán de Heredia, *Las corrientes de espiritualidad entre los Dominicos de Castilla durante la primera mitad del siglo xvi* (Salamanca, 1941).
[3] *Revue de littérature comparée*, XVI (1936), 37 f.

The Italy of Contarini, of Morone and of Flaminio should be methodically interrogated; the religious production of her presses, so abundant, particularly in Venice, should be passed in review, if we wish to study in the right perspective the ascetic-mystic literature of Spain at [this] epoch.[1]

Yet the net can be flung still wider, as Bataillon is indeed fully aware. In all the Catholic spiritual literature of the early sixteenth century there can be detected the powerful influence of Netherlandish and German spiritual traditions—the *devotio moderna*, and the great force of the Carthusians, in particular. Despite the advance of nationalism in this age, the idea of watertight national compartments in Catholic religious influences, capable of being weighed against each other like postal packets, does not correspond to the reality.

Yet if at the outset of the Counter-Reformation it was Spanish and Italian Catholicism, with a strong, more-than-hinted background of Teutonic inspiration in Netherlandish and German spiritual writings, that took the lead; in the seventeenth century the torch was passed to France. The French political and economic recovery after the cessation of the civil wars, the gradual rise of French power against the slow decline of Spanish and Austrian, and the fading of Italian prosperity in the seventeenth century, brought France to the top in religious influence too, in that phenomenal development of Catholic spirituality which Bremond has chronicled,[2] and which did so much to create the ethos of modern Catholic life and to give precision to so many of its features—without which, in fact, modern Catholicism is unimaginable. In the middle decades of the seventeenth century French life experienced a quickening of culture and civilisation, seen, amongst other ways, in the turning of the nobility from arms to culture, the development of the salons, the new role of women in social life, the advance in literary output. These

---

[1] *Ibid.* 39; cf. Bataillon, 'Sur la diffusion des œuvres de Savonarole en Espagne et en Portugal, 1500–1560', in *Mélanges...offerts à M. Joseph Vianey* (Paris, 1934), pp. 93–103; *Erasme et l'Espagne*, pp. 53, 635 ff. I have slightly modified Evennett's translation of the two passages quoted.

[2] H. Bremond, *Histoire littéraire du sentiment religieux en France depuis la fin des guerres de religion jusqu'à nos jours* (12 vols., Paris, 1916–36): English translation of vols. I–III by K. L. Montgomery (London, 1928–36).

civilising, softening qualities appear too, as one would expect, in the French Catholic revival building up on the spade-work of renewal performed in the later decades of the sixteenth century by Jesuits and Capuchins and others. From St Jane Frances Chantal and Madame Acarie through Port Royal to Madame Guyon, the role of women is prominent, though it operates, somehow, with a difference from the role of the Italian nuns, or the Spanish Beatas, in the more drastic life of the sixteenth century; much indeed could be interestingly written of the spiritual influence of women in the Counter-Reformation throughout its course. And here perhaps we can hardly omit a reference to the two phenomena of Jansenism and Quietism, which raise again in the seventeenth-century setting, both inside France and elsewhere, basic problems of theology and of spirituality which had their earlier sixteenth-century counter-reformation analogies: far-reaching problems of Grace, prayer, and the mystical life.

If the problems that I have so far suggested lie mainly around the beginnings of the Counter-Reformation, what are we to say about its end? In about the third quarter of the seventeenth century, the demarcation of territory between Catholicism and the other forms of Christianity that had grown up in the previous 150 years, had, by and large, been stabilised, and though the question of minorities, on both sides, was still often controversial and problematical, direct struggle between the various forms of Christianity—despite the history of James II—no longer held a central position on the stage of European affairs. The fascinating game of periodising post-medieval history is indeed all too easy to play, but it is surely clear that by the end of the seventeenth century changes had come over the mind and face of Europe which marked the working out of the first political and spiritual revolutions of the sixteenth century and the inauguration of a new period—whether we regard this as the period of science, or scepticism, or reason, or of the modern state, or just a new stage in bourgeois capitalism. Similarly, and perhaps necessarily, the process of inner renewal and outward re-adaptation that Catholicism had undergone since about 1500 had reached, speaking broadly, a point of repose, from which a new advance of the same magnitude would not develop until after the French Revolution, when, as at the beginning of the sixteenth century, an apparent moribundity was again to be followed by creative resurrection.

If the Counter-Reformation was, at bottom, the total process of adaptation to new world conditions which Catholicism underwent in the first two centuries of the post-medieval age, a modernisation, in the sense of the establishment of a new 'modus vivendi' of the Church with the world, then it would seem that this effort can be said to have reached an end somewhere in the age of Louis XIV.[1] Despite St John Baptist de la Salle, St Grignon de Montfort, and de Rancé, Bremond suggests that the great creative forces in seventeenth-century French spirituality were coming to their end by the majority of 'Le Roi Soleil'. It is interesting to speculate what new *devotio moderna* a native Dutch or English mode of the Counter-Reformation might have brought to the Catholic Church in the sixteenth and seventeenth centuries, but when all is said and done it remains that, for all the Teutonic influences and manifestations that can be pointed to, the Counter-Reformation drew its main power from the Latin countries, not merely from the energy and creativeness of Renaissance Italy and Renaissance Spain and from the mature French civilisation of the seventeenth century, but from that whole vivid, forceful Mediterranean civilisation of the late sixteenth and early seventeenth centuries which Fernand Braudel's recent book—hailed by Lucien Febvre as a real revolution in historical technique—has emphasised and illuminated in so remarkable a way.[2] Easy generalisations about the decay of Italy owing to the discovery of the sea-route to India, and to the sad consequences of Castilian domination, are apt to overlook what a revitalising boon to the whole of the peninsula was the peace restored in 1559; to ignore how, as such authorities as Cipolla and Braudel now believe, the populations of many of the greater towns in Italy, at any rate in the north and centre, which

---

[1] Cf. Bremond, *Histoire littéraire*, I, xvi.
[2] F. Braudel, *La Méditerranée et le monde méditerranéen à l'époque de Philippe II* (Paris, 1949); Febvre's review repr. in *Pour une histoire à part entière* (Paris, 1962), pp. 167–79.

had been decimated by the wars and diseases of the High Renaissance period, were restored to their late fifteenth-century level by the end of the sixteenth century;[1] or how the trade of the Mediterranean, and the prosperity of Venice and other Italian ports, revived and did not fall before Dutch and English invaders until the early years of the seventeenth century.[2] Of this prosperous Mediterranean culture—of which the idea of an Age of the Baroque is, by itself, an insufficient expression—many manifestations of the Counter-Reformation are evidences and outcomes: such things as the easing of papal finances through the taxable wealth of the now more consolidated papal states; the artistic, political and administrative constructions in Rome from the building of the Gesù and the activities of Sixtus V up to the early eighteenth-century Roman buildings; the promotion from Rome of the Catholic revival in Germany; the foundation in 1622 of the Congregation *de Propaganda Fide*, marking a new extension of Catholic missionary efforts both inside and outside Europe.

Creative, no doubt, in the absolute sense of providing complete and original novelty, in the sense, that is, demanded by Croce in the weighty and penetrating analysis made in his *Storia dell'Età barocca in Italia*,[3] the Counter-Reformation never was, nor in the nature of things could ever have been. But, from its main basis in the Latin world, despite all its limitations, frustrations and imperfections, the Counter-Reformation, by means of all its vigorous activities, ensured the survival into the post-medieval world of a still-persuasive, still-expanding, world form of Christianity under a single centralised control, not broken up into national state-controlled fragments, for all the powers and claims of Catholic monarchs. This is a matter, surely, of the greatest significance for the history of the world, whatever role the modern Catholic Church may be regarded as playing in the

---

[1] Braudel, *op. cit.* p. 272, speaks of 'une très vive poussée démographique' early in the sixteenth century, continued during the second half but rather by 'vitesse acquise'. The reference to Cipolla seems to depend on a letter from Cipolla to Evennett, 27 October 1950, where he cites his own *Profilo di storia demografica della città di Pavia*.

[2] Braudel, *op. cit.* pp. 421–503.

[3] Bari, 1929: see pp. 3–19 for discussion of term 'Controriforma'.

philosophies of the schematic world historians—whether Marx or Spengler or Toynbee. Moreover, both in its spiritual revival as a religion and in its development as an organisation of a political nature, counter-reformation Catholicism showed itself in many ways not a historical changeling but a legitimate product of its historical age; reflecting in its own modes of praying and behaving and organising, more perhaps than in philosophising, the general forces at work in contemporary society. In the lectures that follow I want to try to suggest some ways in which this was so.

## 2

## COUNTER-REFORMATION
## SPIRITUALITY

At the end of my first lecture, I suggested a formula for a possible definition of our subject, namely that in the largest view what we were dealing with was the whole process of adaptation to the post-medieval world of Catholicism—by which expression I mean the religion and organisation of the western medieval Church remaining under Rome. This formula is not intended as a subtle attempt to take the 'counter' out of 'Counter-Reformation' but rather to embrace it within a wider grasp. In stressing the positive, even perhaps, *pace* Croce, the creative side of the movement, we cannot allow ourselves to forget—and indeed it would be flying in the face of history to do so—how vigorously the Counter-Reformation was stimulated in all its aspects and how profoundly it was conditioned by the challenge of Protestantism. The coming into existence of new and competing forms of established Christianity in Europe was one of the things to which adaptation of outlook and policy was needed, and while this brought a new and modernised efficiency in catechismal and controversial methods, and a new impulse to the serious study of Church history, it also served to intensify those habits of caution, suspicion, intransigence, and the appeal to force which are the hallmarks of an anxious defensive, involved in the elaboration and safeguarding of more rigorous definitions. Such traits, indeed, characterised not merely the public relations (as it were) of the Church but also her own internal workings. The inquisitorial principle with all its practical applications—whether in the development of new inquisitorial tribunals proper, or in efforts to control reading, or in other ways—so far from declining towards an ultimate vestigial condition, appropriate to a free community, was strongly felt by authority to be a religious as well as a social necessity. The effect produced on the ecclesiastical attitude towards new intellectual or scientific ideas not in themselves directly concerned with or resulting from religious heresy, could not but be constrictive, and the quasi-tolerance of philosophic and other novelties which marked the Church of the Italian Renaissance came necessarily to be heavily modified. The Church of the Counter-Reformation, indeed, was sufficiently in tune with the age to become and remain acutely conscious that the Catholic conception of Christianity was challenged not merely by the revolutionary, yet still Christian, dogmas of Luther and Calvin, but also by the seeping into the European mind of something more subtle, more deeply burrowing under foundations —a general philosophical scepticism and the nascent ideas of free-thought and rationalism.

Against the attractions which the doctrine of Justification by Faith alone, with all its radical presuppositions and practical consequences, undoubtedly held out for some; against the pull, for the more worldly, of scepticism and hedonism, what had the old Church to offer? The Counter-Reformation could hardly have occurred had it been no more than 'the hastily improvised defence of the vested interests of an archaic ecclesiastical corporation bereft of contemporary or future spiritual significance'.[1] I return with renewed conviction to this sentence written more than fifteen years ago. The Counter-Reformation was first and foremost a powerful religious movement, and it is only by recognising this, not as an afterthought, but as the first condition of a fruitful approach to its study, that we can hope to reduce it to unity and to arrive eventually at some reasonable appraisal. It involved, however, more than the simple reaffirmation of medieval spiritual teachings, and it eventually created a mature spirituality with clear characteristics of its own, on which the impress of the new times and their atmosphere was in many ways clearly discernible.

Yet the spiritual arms and the apostolic technique of the medieval Church in the fifteenth century had not been negligible: preaching abounded in great quantity, though often doubtless of questionable quality, and perhaps of sporadic incidence; the

[1] Evennett, *The Counter-Reformation* (Catholic Truth Society, London, 1935), p. 1.

invention of printing cut both ways—it helped the propagation of Catholic piety and devotion and the preparation for the Counter-Reformation, as well as assisting Protestant propagandists; new devotions and religious practices multiplied rapidly to stimulate the religious feelings of the faithful. Across the century passes a long procession of saints and revivalists, holy women, visionaries, prophets, monastic reformers and the often sincere efforts for ecclesiastical betterment of politicians. The fifteenth century—so full of contradictions—was full of reforms and reformers who between them could not make a Reformation; either in the Catholic or in the Protestant sense. It is not enough, in explanation, to point to the frustrating influence of the papal court whence came a flood of dispensations and exemptions cutting across the efforts of the reformers, a worldly outlook, all the obstructions and disappointments inevitable in a highly organised administrative central machine, and a preoccupation with culture, politics and finance. The essential sterility and ephemerality—in the long view—of all reform movements between the Council of Constance and the pontificate of Paul III proceeded in the last analysis from the tiredness of generations which seemed to have lost the art of creation, or re-creation, in so many spheres of human activity; which could produce neither a Loyola nor a Luther; which could not summon the strength of will to deal radically with the condition of affairs which the embedding of all ecclesiastical offices, from the highest to the lowest, in the social, financial and economic structure of society had led to. It is as if the more virile psychology and willpower of a new, less worn-out generation of men was required for the seeds of reform, already so widely present in the fifteenth century, to strike deep roots and acquire a true power of effective and lasting growth. If religion is an essential ingredient in men's lives, it is perhaps no surprise that stronger purpose and a more lasting staying-power should have appeared in their spiritual strivings simultaneously with the manifestation of a new masterfulness and freedom in their politics and other secular activities. Without questioning the practical abilities of many fifteenth-century characters, new ability and determination seem nonetheless to have come into the blood of the generation born in the later years of the fifteenth century—for what reason, history by itself can perhaps hardly determine. And with men of the stamp of the Cortes, the Michael-angelos, the Ferdinands of Aragon, the Henry VIIIs, there appeared also the Luthers and Zwinglis, the Cajetans, Carafas and Loyolas. Contemporaneously with the discovery of America and the sea route to the East, with the quick conquests of the new political spirit in the European states, with the gradual evolution in Luther's mind of his new religious outlook, there were also being formed, among the many possible seed-beds of a more powerful Catholic religious revival, certain germinating centres of a new spiritual urgency and compelling example, which would supply the first spear-heads of the 'Counter-Reformation'.

If we scan the period from Columbus's first voyages to the sack of Rome—after which the Roman court first began to apply itself in seriousness to the question of reform—several such centres can be noted. In Italy many associations, or oratories, half lay, half clerical, had been formed in a number of cities, not only for the cultivation of a more intense and lasting piety among their members, but also for the performance of urgent charitable works, the care of orphans, the education of the poor, and most of all the institution of hospitals, principally for sufferers from the new disease of syphilis, regarded as incurable, brought in, it was said, by the French, and which most ordinary hospitals would not deal with. Here much was due to the influence of St Catherine of Genoa,[1] a lay woman, and her disciple and biographer Ettore Vernazza, and from Genoa derived the Oratory of Divine Love in Rome which ran a hospital for *incurabili* and whence came the four founders of the Theatine Congregation of reformed priests and their first novice. Similar circles existed in many other centres. Those in Brescia and the surrounding district have recently been studied by Cistellini;[2] from this group came St Angela Merici. In Venice the group represented

---

[1] See *Enciclopedia cattolica*, III, 1145–8; and more generally Pastor, *History of the Popes*, X, chs. 12–13; XI, ch. 13; Evennett, *New Cambridge Modern History*, II, 285–90, and works cited above, p. 13, n. 5.

[2] A. Cistellini, *Figure della riforma pretridentina* (Brescia, 1948).

by Contarini and his friends is held to have had a continuous existence stretching back to Ludovico Barbo, the early fifteenth-century reformer of the Italian Benedictines and the founder of the Congregation of Sta Justina of Padua.[1] The rather freer Naples group is well known. The cult and influence, too, of Savonarola were strong and persistent, long after his death, producing notable effects—if we are to believe Marcel Bataillon and Fr Beltrán de Heredia[2]—on both the Spanish and the north Italian Dominicans, especially the latter: from these came a remarkable spiritual leader, John Baptist Carioni, better known as Fra Battista da Crema, author of the widely read *Vittoria di se stesso* and spiritual director of some of the men who made the earliest foundations of clerks regular in Italy.[3] Thus, though lay was mixed with clerical inspiration in these numerous Italian circles, the traditional inspiration of friars and monks was by no means lacking; and side by side with the work, so lay in original concept, of St Angela Merici, there was the remarkable influence of enclosed contemplative nuns such as Laura Mignani, the Augustinian canoness, the confidant of St Cajetan; the Dominican Blessed Stefana Quinzani; and others. It was into the cloisters of Camaldoli that the earliest Venetian friends of Contarini went; while the primitive Franciscan spirit—never wholly dead at any time in Italy—was germinating again in Mateo da Bascia and his followers who canalised his aspirations into the renewed apostolic and ascetical fervour of the Capuchin order. In Spain and France and Germany as well as Italy the observant branches of Franciscans and Dominicans and other friars were making headway, and there are some remarkable chapters in the history of the reformed Preachers in Spain related by Fr Beltrán de Heredia.[4] Luther came from a strictly observant, not a lax, branch of the Augustinians. More powerful in the north was the influence of the German Carthusians,

---

[1] On Barbo, *Enciclopedia cattolica*, II, 830-1.
[2] Works cited above, pp. 17, nn. 2, 3, and 18, n. 1.
[3] *Enciclopedia cattolica*, II, 1049-50, referring to O. Premoli, *Fra Battista da Crema secondo documenti inediti* (Rome, 1910), etc.
[4] *Historia de la reforma de la Provincia de España* (? Madrid, 1939). General accounts in H. Jedin, *History of the Council of Trent* I, (London, 1957), 139-45, with bibliography p. 140; Aubenas and Ricard, *L'Eglise et la Renaissance*, pp. 275-311.

especially the Charterhouse of Cologne, which kept alive the spirit of northern Catholic piety that owed so much to the Canons of Windesheim and the Brethren of the Common Life, with their traditions of new devotion and regular meditative prayer.[1] Even in the south, where Valladolid and Montserrat, Chezal-Benoît and Subiaco had led or were leading Benedictine revivals, these northern influences were powerful. Spanish translations of Ludolph, the Saxon Carthusian, of Thomas à Kempis, and others of the northerners, were abroad in Spain before 1500 and certainly in the early decades of the sixteenth century, when the Basque gentleman Iñigo de Loyola was beginning his extraordinary career.

In all these quarters, and no doubt others, we find, not self-conscious and ambitious programmes for the reform of the Church as a whole but, what was more necessary for that reform, the taking up, refertilising and modernising by men of outstanding spiritual fibre, of the disciplines of prayer, self-control, and charitable activity, whether as individuals or in community life, in the personal search for the Kingdom of God, and for the good of their neighbours. No doubt, however, these were as yet small oases, in an enormous area where the most lamentable deficiencies and abuses existed. None of these groups or individuals whom I have mentioned seems to have been conscious of being influenced by what was happening in Germany and Switzerland, the import and permanence of which were for long misunderstood and underestimated in Italy. And yet all their efforts might have been as ephemeral as those of their fifteenth-century predecessors had they not become caught up in a more general organised movement of urgency and enthusiasm; and for the formation and correlation of this, under the aegis of the papacy, the fear of what was occurring in Germany was indeed, ultimately, largely responsible. The Counter-Reformation, helping to give self-conscious unified shape to the Catholic reform, may perhaps be said to have properly come into existence under the pontificate of Paul III. And yet no amount of unity of control

[1] Jedin, *History of the Council of Trent*, I, 143–5; L. Cognet, *De la dévotion moderne à la spiritualité française*, (Paris, 1958), ch. 1.

or direction, or stimulus of fear, would have guaranteed permanency or success unless there had also been present the necessary spiritual basis. The spirituality of the counter-reformation Church, its roots deep in the past, developed nevertheless under the pressure of outward circumstances.

In its gradual formation, against the evolving background of the Protestant revolution, the spiritual revival and transformation of Catholicism took, inevitably, more rigid forms than might otherwise have been the case, or than might have been anticipated in the earlier stages, before the humanist ways of thought had become suspect and Lutheranism had crystallised. Books and teachings accepted as valuable in the 1520s found themselves condemned in the more cautious and harsher 1550s, when certain spiritual issues had become fundamentally clearer. The powerful attractions of the idea of Justification by Faith alone, of the new conception of Faith itself, and of the view of Justification as—broadly speaking—imputed rather than actually attained, were not limited to those who ultimately followed the lead of Martin Luther. To many, a comfortable feeling of absolute assurance in God alone, a relief from the continuous strain of effort and conflict in the spiritual life, the removal of all the complicated paraphernalia of Church obligations and the artificial multiplication of sins *quia prohibita*, may well have appeared, in the conditions of the early sixteenth century, as the revelation of a new and purely spiritual religion. But even among certain men of intellectual eminence and real spiritual maturity, who saw the full implications of Fra Martin's revolutionary theology, a stronger emphasis on the part played in man's salvation by freely given divine Grace, as contrasted with his own feeble strivings, was regarded as desirable for a better balanced Catholic spiritual life. Six years before the outbreak of the Indulgence controversy made Luther's theology a subject of public debate, Gasparo Contarini, the eminent Venetian man of affairs (who had not followed his friends Giustiniani, Quirini and Georgi into the cloister of Camaldoli) underwent at his Easter Confession of 1511 a spiritual experience which impressed upon him a new and enduring illumination of the meaning of

God's Justice, and which so responsible a Catholic historian as Professor Jedin has recently compared to the famous, if perhaps somewhat elusive, 'experience' of Luther, while reminding us, however, that in Contarini's case the experience was one in connection with a sacrament and not in implied hostility to the sacramental principle.[1] The attitude of soul for which Contarini stood and which was shared by many eminent and sincere Catholics, such as Morone, Seripando, Pole, Flaminio, Gropper[2] —to take a few eminent names—and by a penumbra of more freely speculating believers like Juan de Valdés[3] and his circle, may be regarded as an attempt to provide, within the framework of traditional Catholicism, for some reasonable element of the new religious attitude to which Luther's odyssey and the popularity of his doctrine bore witness.

Fine-spun speculations about the nature of God's Justice and the operation of his Grace in relation to individual men freely seeking him, may well, when reduced to the dry expressions of theological terminology, seem academic and unreal. But behind the various complicated theories of Justification which were flung at each other in the many conferences and controversies of the early sixteenth century, there lay—as later there lay behind the terminology of casuistry which Pascal ridiculed—matters known and felt to be of vital importance for the spiritual life of Christians and the salvation of immortal souls. Professor Jedin, in the first volume of his new *History of the Council of Trent*, has emphasised the extreme importance, in regard to the eventual drafting in 1547 of the Tridentine decrees on Justification, of the exhaustive controversies of the previous thirty years, in which the root theological issue that divided Protestantism from Catholicism had been brought out.[4] In that decree the various half-way houses towards Lutheranism put forward by Contarini,

---

[1] 'Ein 'Turmerlebnis' des jungen Contarini', *Historisches Jahrbuch*, LXX (1951), 115–30.

[2] For Seripando, see above, p. 10, n. 2; for others, see *Enciclopedia cattolica*, under names.

[3] *Ibid.* XII, 964, with references.

[4] Jedin, *History of the Council of Trent*, I, 409, n. 7, and in general 355–409; for Tridentine debates and decree, *ibid.* II (London, 1961), book iii, chs. 5, 7 and 8; *Seripando*, chs. 5, 20–2.

Seripando, Gropper, and others who felt the pull towards a more Augustinian theology were rejected. This fact, vital for the history of counter-reformation theology, is of necessity equally vital for the formation of its spirituality, for spirituality must be based on theological correctness if it is to avoid the disaster of mere self-illusion. Even before 1547—while it could still be maintained that uncertainty about orthodoxy existed—the authorities were much concerned to detect and check any apparent tendencies towards the false mysticism that they felt would be involved in any kind of approach towards the principle of the rejection of works as an essential ingredient in the attainment of salvation. After 1547, however, uncertainty was at an end, and one of the foundation-stones of counter-reformation spirituality was irrevocably laid.

The theological definitions of the Council of Trent in regard to Grace, while not rendering impossible such later phenomena as Baianism, the Molina-Bañez controversy 'de Auxiliis', or Jansenism, were nevertheless sufficiently clear and comprehensive to provide both a basis and a framework for the development of the new devotional movements and spiritual techniques of the hour. They afforded no true grounds for that hostility towards contemplative prayer and mysticism which the related fears of Lutheranism and Illuminism implanted, justifiably or unjustifiably, so deeply in the minds of many of the ablest and most devoted Catholic reformers. Nevertheless, the view that Justification by Faith alone must logically lead to Illuminism or quasi-mystical aberrations was widely held, especially in Spain. It may well have done an injustice to the essentially unmystical Martin Luther, who, we are told by Mr Rupp, 'drove himself nearly daft...trying to follow the mystic counsels of St Bonaventura, until his own commonsense bade him desist'.[1] In these circumstances, the effect of the Tridentine decrees was to make doubly sure in practice that the spirituality of the Counter-Reformation would be one in which activity of all kinds was to play a very large part; in which active striving after self-control and the acquisition of virtues would be vital; in which zeal for good

[1] Gordon Rupp, *Luther's progress to the Diet of Worms* (London, 1951), p. 28.

works of mercy and charity, and labour for the salvation of souls, were to predominate: a spirituality which was to reflect the bustle and energy and determination of sixteenth-century man, feeling at last that he had a power over himself and over things, to be applied, in the Counter-Reformation, for the greater glory of God and the revival of his Church. The spirituality of the Counter-Reformation sprang from a triple alliance, as it were, between the Tridentine clarifications of the orthodox teaching on Grace and Justification, the practical urge of the day towards active works, and certain new developments in ascetical teaching and practice which promoted this outlook. These developments had been taking place slowly during the previous hundred and fifty years, but were now brought to a head and popularised according to the practical needs of the time and the particular religious climate generated by the necessities of the counter-reformation struggles. I am referring here chiefly to the systematisation of the meditative form of mental prayer, which was much cultivated in the fifteenth century, in the first instance as a way towards the reform of monastic and clerical life. Thence it was adapted progressively to the requirements of the devout layman, to become eventually, through the agency of the great spiritual masters of the sixteenth and seventeenth centuries—Ignatius, Scupoli, François de Sales, Bérulle, Vincent de Paul—one of the cornerstones of the new and reinvigorated spirituality that was gradually diffused, by means of all the new apostolic techniques of the Counter-Reformation, throughout the whole Catholic Church.

The late Henri Watrigant, of the Society of Jesus, in a series of articles designed as a chapter in a projected history of meditation, examined very fully the history of the development of the art and practice of meditation in the late fourteenth and the fifteenth centuries.[1] He distinguished between two main sources of the movement: first, the writers and teachers of the *devotio moderna* in the Low Countries and north-western Germany;

---

[1] 'La méditation méthodique et l'école des Frères de la Vie Commune', and 'La méditation méthodique et Jean Mauburnus', *Revue d'ascétique et de mystique*, III (1922), 134 f. and IV (1923), 13 f.; 'La genèse des Exercices de Saint Ignace de Loyola', *Etudes*, LXXI (1897), 506 f.; LXXII, 195 f.; LXXIII, 199 f.

and, secondly, the Franciscan and Carthusian traditions, behind which lay, of course, a long earlier history of doctrines and practices of prayer, partly meditative, partly mystical in nature. It is a great injustice to suppose—as some seem to[1]—that there was nothing more to the spirituality of the *devotio moderna* than sensible, or superficial, devotion based, consciously or unconsciously, on a nominalist intellectual agnosticism. The series of writings and influences that from 1370 onwards emanated from the Brethren of the Common Life and the Canons of Windesheim, and those under their influence, and which formed an important source of counter-reformation Catholicism, were far from being concerned exclusively with the promotion of sensible devotion— with merely 'affective' religion, as the spiritual authors say. It is worth while recalling the names of some of these men whose collective, cumulative influence was so widespread and so lasting: Gerard Groote himself, founder of the Brethren of the Common Life; Florent Radewijns, his disciple; Lubert Berner; Peter Gerlach; Gerard of Zutphen; Jan Goossens Vos van Heusden, prior of Windesheim; Henry of Mande; Thomas à Kempis; Jan Mombaer—the *catena* stretches from the last decades of the fourteenth century to the death of Mombaer in Paris in 1520.[2] Of the writers mentioned, Père Watrigant picks out three who were specially prominent by the didactic and systematic nature of their writings and the way in which they developed the whole art of meditation, systematically setting out in orderly method the manner of meditation, arranging meditations in groups, or set exercises, or for periods of time, by the day, the week or the month; or in ascending grades—ladders of ascent, *scalae*. These three were Radewijns, Gerard of Zutphen and Jan Mombaer, whose bulky *Rosetum* is an enormous compendium of various treatises on prayer of different types. These three, incidentally, were all men with a university training.

Closely connected with these, and other representatives of

---

[1] I am not sure who is intended here, though it is possibly Hugo Rahner (cf. Postscript, p. 128); cf. also Jedin, *History of the Council of Trent*, I, 145.

[2] See Jedin, *ibid.*, with bibliography; R. R. Post, *De moderne devotie* (Amsterdam, 1940), esp. pp. 132–47. A. Hyma, *The Christian Renaissance: a history of the 'Devotio Moderna'* (New York, 1925), seems undiscriminating. See Postscript, pp. 126–8.

the *devotio moderna*, who figure in Joannes Busch's contemporary history of the devotion and of the monastic reformers associated with it, were influences deriving from older traditions—principally Carthusian and Franciscan: Henry of Kalkar, the Carthusian teacher of Groote himself, Henry of Hesse, Denys, Ludolph the Saxon, and other Carthusians; among the Franciscans, the traditions derived from St Bonaventure were carried on by Otto of Passau, David of Augsburg, Ubertino of Casale, Henry Herp —'Harpius'—who died at Malines in 1478 and whose work became suspect in the more astringent atmosphere of the middle sixteenth century.[1] Other more individualistic writers added their contributions, such as Pierre d'Ailly and Gerson, Tauler and Ruysbroeck the mystics, Johann de Rode, the German Benedictine reformer.

There emerged from all these writings, among other things, the elaboration and gradual popularisation of a systematic method of private, meditative prayer which exercised a wide and profound influence. A 'science' of meditation came into being with its own rules and principles, which if regularly and systematically observed, was eminently calculated to strengthen, in each individual, habits of self-control, perseverance in the struggle for virtue, and the maintenance of that sense of continuous self-dedication so essential to monasticism. This method of personal self-improvement was much cultivated in the monastic, and especially the Benedictine, reforms of the fifteenth century, not indeed in opposition to liturgical or corporate acts of worship such as the recitation of the divine office in choir, or the general ceremonial of the Church, but in a complementary though in a certain sense also a contradistinctive way. Italy and Spain, as well as Germany, felt the impulse of this northern spiritual influence which brought order and staying-power, as well as a new devotional warmth and what the Germans call *Innerlichkeit*, into monastic spirituality. It is highly probable that Netherland influences were at work in the early fifteenth century in Venice, among the reformed canons of St George of Alga, whence there

---

[1] Accounts of most of these will be found in Cognet, *De la dévotion moderne à la spiritualité française*, ch. I.

came to Padua Ludovico Barbo, founder of the Benedictine congregation of Sta Justina, and author of the *Modus meditandi et orandi*.[1] Centres of Benedictine reform so far apart as Subiaco, Valladolid, Bursfeld and Melk are said, on more or less circumstantial evidence, to have been influenced in a similar way, and, in spite of Benedictine authors who take a different view, it would appear that even so eminent a Spanish work as the Book of Exercises for the Spiritual Life—the *Ejercitatorio de la Vida Espiritual*—of Abbot García Cisneros of Montserrat, though in form and purpose no doubt a true original work, was in its substance almost entirely taken from the northern authors of the previous hundred years.[2] A more subtle problem of derivation, as we shall see later, is raised by the other great Spanish work in which the systematic elaboration of formal meditation comes, in some respects, to its climax—the *Spiritual Exercises* of St Ignatius.

Barbo, Cisneros, and most of the authors of the *devotio moderna* wrote specifically for monks. Their works presuppose the monastic routine. But the self-control, attention to prayer, perseverance in virtue, and sense of dedication that are underlined in the religious life, apply in some degree to all Christians, and it was eventually the wider task and destiny of this movement of ordered, meditative prayer, woven into the traditional doctrine of the three ways or stages of the spiritual life—purgative, illuminative and unitive—and logically expounded by recognised masters, to become one of the most important spiritual arms of the Counter-Reformation to the reform of laity and clergy alike. We should notice here, however, that in the eyes of its greatest exponents in the fifteenth and early sixteenth centuries, the cultivation of systematic, mental-image-forming meditation

---

[1] Post, *De moderne devotie*, p. 137, remarks the parallel, but is not clear who influences whom; cf. Postscript, p. 128.

[2] *Dictionnaire de spiritualité*, II (Paris, 1953), 910–21; A. Albareda, 'Intorno alla scuola di orazione metodica stabilita a Monserrato dall'Abate Garsias Jimenez de Cisneros', *Archivum historicum Societatis Jesu*, xxv (1956), 254–316. I have not seen G. M. Colombás, *Un reformador benedictino en tiempo de los Reyes Católicos: García Jiménez de Cisneros, abad de Montserrat* (Montserrat, 1955), who (Albareda, p. 316) suggests a meeting between Cisneros and Standonck and Mombaer in Paris in 1496. See Postscript, p. 128.

no more excluded the possibility for some souls of a higher type of contemplative mystical prayer than it condemned, either for monks or for laymen, vocal prayer either private or communal.

All this technique of regular mental prayer with its demands on the powers of the mind and its requirements in the way of preparatory and concomitant asceticism, was conceived and practised in highly individualistic terms, to the diminution of stress on communal or liturgical values. Surely, we see here the individualism of the age taking its appropriate form in Catholic spirituality—something, perhaps, not wholly unconnected with the process by which, as medieval society dissolved, the mystic interpenetration of Church and society faded and the individual was left to face by itself the problem raised by the mutual confrontation of Church and state as separate perfect societies. The loyalty to the Church which the Counter-Reformation demanded does not seem to have inspired a clear reaffirmation of the doctrine of the Church as the mystical body of Christ in such a way as to make this the basis of a new corporate 'mystic'. The central position of the individual in the practice of counter-reformation spirituality was, admittedly, radically different both from the moral view of his position in the purely humanist ideology and from the theological view of his position in the Protestant scheme of things. Less Pelagian on the one hand than the extreme humanist concepts which exalted the complete self-sufficiency and self-responsibility of the independent human being, it nevertheless rejected the Protestant doctrine of the nature and results of original sin which to some, at any rate, seemed to make nonsense of humanist principles. The counter-reformation doctrine of Christian struggle and effort, laborious, long, chequered, perilous, but aided, fostered and eased by systematic precepts and counsels representing accumulated wisdom and experience, announced that Man—even in face of his Almighty Creator—carried, to some extent, his own fate in his own hands.

But this was, however, only half the story. God would respond to man if man responded to him; the process was mutual and cumulative (I am not using technical theological terms). If

the great achievements of the Counter-Reformation, in the spirit
as well as in action, rest to a large extent upon the doctrine of
ceaseless effort and combat against self; over against this, in
necessary complementation, stands the conviction that in another
sense it is God who does all, and that in the ultimate analysis
his glory is all that matters. Not for nothing was the motto of
the Society of Jesus—for all its perhaps sometimes exaggerated
stress on action—*Ad Majorem Dei Gloriam*. Hence, the spiritual
leaders of the Counter-Reformation, without exception, turned
back zealously to the covenanted channels of God's Grace, as
an essential factor in the new bursting of spiritual energy—the
sacramental system which the doctrine of Justification by Faith
alone had so deeply undermined. A more than annual Confession
and Communion for serious lay people, a more nearly daily
celebration of Mass for priests and bishops, became a note of
the reformers in all Catholic countries.[1] The sacrament of Confession was henceforth to be not merely the annual preparation
for the reception of Easter Communion, but a regular occurrence
in the devout life and in the spiritual combat, linked closely
with the technique of regular examination of conscience and
the practice of fruitful pious meditation on the life of Christ or
other biblical or devotional themes. The confessional became
more and more a regular rather than an exceptional resource, and
inevitably there came a great advance in the science of confessors,
in the whole role of the spiritual director, and therefore also in
the development of moral theology, of cases of conscience—in
a word, of casuistry. This was an inevitable part of the process,
regrettable only when abused. Such a doctrine as probabilism,
with all its variations and intricacies, serves to show the length
to which a zeal to help Christians by a careful definition of sin,
admittedly in a perhaps somewhat legalistic manner, could be
carried, in the attempts to clarify and compose consciences.

And if the sacrament of Confession held in Catholic religious
life of 1600 or 1650 a place totally different from that which it

[1] On frequent Communion, see *Dictionnaire de théologie catholique*, III, 515–52,
esp. 531 f.: note approval of Zaccaria, Gaetano da Thiene and Ignatius; strong
reserve of Domingo de Soto, Azpilcueta. I have found nothing very helpful on
Confession.

had held in 1400, similar great changes had come over eucharistic piety. The middle ages adored the host at Mass, but outside the liturgy did not pay to it, when reserved, the outward reverence paid in Catholic churches today, nor was it made the centre of non-liturgical devotions. The non-liturgical worship of the host in the service of benediction, in the forty hours' exposition,[1] and by practices such as modern 'visits' is a counter-reformation development. Much popularised by the Capuchins and Jesuits, the forty hours' exposition was first performed in 1527, in Milan, in order to invoke divine aid during a time of war and plague; and the growth of devotions to the blessed sacrament as the abiding sacramental presence of Christ in his Church is wholly a characteristic of modern Catholicism. But it is equally true and certainly no less important that the spirituality of the Counter-Reformation also restored to a much more central place in Christian life the prime purpose of the Eucharist as a divine food in which Christ is given to each individual. It is extremely difficult to form an overall picture of the frequency of Communion in about the year 1500. While many bishops and priests, especially those without care of souls, said Mass only very infrequently, daily Mass, or Mass several times a week, was generally the mark of the reformed monastic communities of the age, or even of the normally observant; it certainly became a mark of the new sixteenth-century congregations. Among the laity, and clergy other than priests, reception of the holy eucharist was much less frequent. The exhortations of theologians do not seem to have been much implemented by the efforts of parochial pastors. But pious circles even in the fifteenth century practised a more frequent recourse than the obligatory annual. At the Collège de Montaigu in the University of Paris, which had felt the influence of the Flemish reformers Standonck and Mombaer—and every reader of the *Imitation of Christ*, in full, knows Thomas à Kempis's views!—fortnightly Communion was practised at the time of St Ignatius's stay there about 1530. St Ignatius in his early days communicated, and counselled pious souls to

---

[1] See articles, 'Quarantore', in *Enciclopedia cattolica*, X, 376–8, and 'Forty Hours' Devotion' (Thurston), in *Catholic Encyclopedia*, VI, 151–3.

communicate, weekly. Two or three times weekly was laid down for Jesuit scholastics, and was probably the norm among fervent unordained clerics. But the precise frequency with which a man or woman might presume with fruit and without fear of sacrilege to approach the holy table was a matter for direction; and the views of directors might differ, as indeed the practice in convents and lay confraternities varied. Though the Counter-Reformation saw the restoration of Holy Communion as a more integral part of regular Christian life and spiritual 'technique', nothing like the free daily Communion of the twentieth century was either advised or practised, in general, so far as laymen were concerned.[1] So far as generalisation can be hazarded, the daily celebration of Mass by priests probably became very widespread throughout the Church in the sixteenth and seventeenth centuries—the gradual spread and perfection of seminary training would probably bring this about—while monthly or weekly Communion was frequently permitted to lay people who took the practice of religion with regular seriousness, who had embarked on the devout life.[2] In all Catholic countries, especially Italy, eucharistic societies and brotherhoods sprang up. Yet there may have been some falling back in the late seventeenth century, perhaps as the indirect influence of Jansenism, which tended to regard the act of Communion—and indeed the celebration of Mass itself—more as a kind of recognition of merit acquired than as a help towards acquiring it. Early in the seventeenth century, however, the Spanish Carmelite nun, Anne of Jesus, was surprised at the extent of frequent Communion in Paris, and records the surprise of Parisians that the Spanish Carmelite nuns who introduced Carmel into France did not communicate more frequently. But in his account of the great abbesses who reformed so many of the French Benedictine nunneries about the turn of the sixteenth century, Bremond points out the significance of the fact that it

---

[1] But cf. Ignatius to Teresa Rejadella, 15 November 1543, in H. Rahner, *St. Ignatius Loyola: letters to women* (Freiburg/Edinburgh, 1960), pp. 338 f., where he approves the suggestion, admittedly of a nun, that she should receive Communion daily.

[2] G. le Bras, *Introduction à l'histoire de la pratique religieuse en France*, I (Paris, 1942), 96, does not suggest any sign of a general eucharistic piety in France in the 17th and 18th centuries; he is chiefly concerned with rural Catholicism.

was often the introduction of mental prayer which led the nuns to greater frequentation of the sacraments.[1] There was in fact a necessary and close connection between the personal discipline involved in regular periods of daily mental prayer and the new fervour for the sacraments of Confession and Communion. These two aspects of counter-reformation piety—the efforts of personal *ascèse*, the 'disciplined life of religious regularity', and the recourse to the covenanted channels whence flowed divine Grace *ex opere operato*—are seen once more to come together.

The revival of the sacramental life, the spread and development of powerful new techniques of meditative prayer and eucharistic devotions, the driving urge towards outward activity and good works as a factor in personal sanctification, all deployed, as it were, within the framework of Tridentine doctrine; here I suggest are the essential elements of Counter-Reformation spirituality, as formulated and taught by a succession of spiritual geniuses of the highest order throughout the sixteenth and seventeenth centuries, transforming and enormously quickening the spiritual life-blood of Catholicism, eventuating in a new creative efflorescence of institutions, and new reorganisations of the practical working and administration of the Church, in a word the beginnings of modern Catholicism. Within this formula we see, of course, ebbs and flows, variations of emphasis, a variety of spirits, according to nation, tradition, religious order, precise period or play of circumstances. It would be as much out of touch with reality to suggest the early attainment of a rigid uniformity as it would be to forget that for long the new intensification of devotion was seen and felt only in limited circles and that the name of *chietini* for the new class of *dévots* (revealing the impression made by the Theatines) persisted for decades in Italy and Spain. Again, the whole French spirituality of the seventeenth century, for example, in so far as it derived from Bérulle, had a distinctive Christocentric character;[2] while the intensive and exclusive concentration on formal discursive meditation with its mental efforts, and on the principle of activity

---

[1] *Histoire littéraire du sentiment religieux*, II (1921), 440; pp. 436–41 were clearly very important for Evennett here.    [2] For Bérulle, see Postscript, pp. 139–41.

and struggle—of which the Jesuits were the supreme and the extreme champions—was questioned in a running undertone of dissatisfaction by upholders of a more contemplative doctrine of prayer, not only in Spain, but elsewhere too. In Italy the severe ascetic spirit of St Charles Borromeo, and of the influential *Combattimento Spirituale* of the Theatine Lorenzo Scupoli was in full accord with the new tide; St Philip Neri and the warmer spirit of the Oratorians—not indeed indulgent but somehow modishly Franciscan—represented a variation that found a wide response in the Rome of Sixtus V, Clement VIII and Paul V which St Philip did so much to convert. The Dominican spiritual influence, widespread and powerful everywhere in the sixteenth century, was not wholly in step with that of the Society of Jesus; the soon ubiquitous Capuchins had a way of their own; the methods of St François de Sales were distinctive.

Nevertheless, it is not invalid to recognise in the dominant spirituality of the Counter-Reformation certain powerful and distinctive traits. Broadly speaking, its genius took individual rather than corporate or liturgical expressions. It was highly sacramental; not biblical, in the Protestant sense of a personal formation based primarily on direct reading of Scripture, its great masters were all impregnated with the Bible and its meditative practices were largely focused on the life and passion of Christ; while the humanity of Christ, which fifteenth-century devotions such as the rosary and the cult of St Anne had emphasised, was the object of increased veneration. It was exacting, in that it demanded continuous heroic effort at prayer and self-control and self-improvement and good works; practical, in that it closely linked active good works and self-improvement, and assumed the placing of a high value on the former in the sight of God for Justification, and also in that, at any rate with the Jesuits, asceticism was kept within reasonable bounds. It may be rated humanistic in that it proceeded on the belief that each man's destiny for all eternity was partly in his own power to make or mar. The whole trend—even, as Professor Jedin has remarked, among the Carthusians[1]—was away from contemplation

[1] *History of the Council of Trent*, I, 144.

towards apostolate. And for many of those traits there can be no doubt that the conditions of the time were in a sense partly responsible: all that was implied in the challenge of the Reformation, in the challenge of the discovery of new races of men to be evangelised, the challenge where it occurred of a hostile state, even perhaps the less obvious but in the long run more far-reaching challenge to the whole Christian concept latent in the germs of secularism and free-thought.

Such was, in its main characteristics, I think, the spirituality on which was based the religious formation given in the Tridentine seminaries, especially those under Jesuit management, prevalent among many of the new congregations and the reformed older orders, and given to thousands of devout laity under spiritual directors in the sixteenth and seventeenth centuries. Of this active, virile, exacting religious outlook of counter-reformation Catholicism, with all its strengths as well as with what it had of weakness and insufficiency, the Jesuits were the outstanding representatives. It was because they were so fully representative of all its main characteristics, so fully aware of all the supreme urgent necessities of the new epoch and its new climate—so far as the preservation and expansion of Catholicism were concerned—that they became the outstanding force in the whole counter-reformation movement; that they became its modernisers (to avoid the overtones of the word modernist) to the extent even of incurring the charge of opportunism, in so many spheres; and that, lastly, the Society of Jesus, while retaining its own peculiar exclusiveness of spirit as a 'close corporation', paradoxically enough succeeded in impressing so much of its own principles, outlook and ethos on so many sides and parts of Catholic life and organisation.

In my next lecture I shall be concerned with St Ignatius and the Spiritual Exercises as the source of the spirituality of the Society of Jesus.

# 3

## ST. IGNATIUS AND THE
## SPIRITUAL EXERCISES

I attempted in my last lecture the somewhat formidable task of trying to convey what seem to me to be the main characteristics which marked the reinvigoration of Catholic spiritual life during the Counter-Reformation: the main traits of that teaching in regard to spirituality which gradually prevailed in the formation of new generations of parochial clergy in the Tridentine seminaries, in the pastoral activities of religious orders and new congregations of priests, and which was passed down to the laity in multiple ways throughout the sixteenth and seventeenth centuries, to the general moral reform of the Church in head and members. Among these agents of spiritual renewal, for both clergy and laity, the Society of Jesus was of outstanding and, in the true sense of the word, peculiar importance; and its teaching and influence in the spiritual sphere show almost all the characteristic counter-reformation marks to the highest degree. The Tridentine decree on Justification had shut out the Augustinian, or if you like, semi-Lutheran tendencies evinced by Contarini, Seripando, Pole, Gropper and others: the Jesuits developed a theological school concerning the relations of free will with Grace which, with the great controversy with the Dominicans over Molina's work, brought upon them the reproach of swinging to the near verge of Pelagianism. Bound up with this was their constant stress on activity of all kinds; the active use of the mind and intellect, with all their powers, in prayer, and especially in pictorial meditation, as against contemplative trends; their doctrine of the insufficiency of purely passive resistance to temptation with its corollary of the necessary counter-attack, the principle of *agendo contra*; the development of their casuistry in a humane and accommodating direction; their respect for

43

each individual and his 'special case', seen in the flexibility of their general spiritual direction; their reaction from excessive corporal mortifications, either for themselves or their penitents. Active struggle against self; activity on behalf of others; frequent recourse to the sacraments; prayer found in work and action in the world rather than in eremetical retirement from it: these were some hallmarks.

Within the Counter-Reformation, however, the Jesuits were themselves a 'special case' in that, while breathing the same general spiritual atmosphere as others in the movement, they nevertheless depended immediately, for their formation, on a personality and a teaching about both of which there was something of the unique, and as a result of which the Society of Jesus, while generating and retaining its own peculiar exclusiveness of spirit, nevertheless became the most powerful, active, modernising, humanistic, and flexible force in the Counter-Reformation, impressing, in the long run, so much of its outlook and even to some extent the principles of its structural form on the life and organisation of Catholicism as a whole.

The small international society of the first nine—'Haec minima congregatio'—which was approved by the papacy in 1540 and which took up its headquarters in Rome, putting itself at the special disposition of the papacy because of its international character, had as its object the salvation and perfection not only of its own members, but equally those of other men. It was a society of reformed and apostolic priests. It had two special and outstanding assets, apart from the high qualities of all its original members: they were the remarkable history and gifts of its founder, Ignatius of Loyola; and the Spiritual Exercises which he had constructed and worked out as a technique for conversion. Applied first to his own original companions, they were soon to reach a much wider public, and to become the foundation of Jesuit pastoral activity, in preaching, missions, retreats, personal direction and otherwise. Not every point in the formation and early history of the Society, and the place of the Exercises in it, is by any means historically crystal-clear; but that the Exercises are inextricably linked up with St Ignatius's personality and evolution and with the foundation and development of the Society is hardly open to question.

Let us look then, first, at these 'Exercises'—the full title, in English, is: *Spiritual Exercises whereby to conquer oneself and order one's life without being influenced in one's decision by any inordinate affection.* The text of the *Spiritual Exercises* of St Ignatius does not constitute a continuous book intended to be read through as such and used by the individual who hopes to profit by them. The work is not a literary treatise on the spiritual life, or even a special didactic treatise on meditation, to be consulted at her own fireside, as it were, by the fervent soul seeking light on the amendment of life and the approach to God. The Spiritual Exercises are a special experience to be undergone, a shock-tactic spiritual gymnastic to be undertaken and performed under guidance, at some particular moment— perhaps of inward crisis—when new decisions and resolutions in life are called for or held to be desirable. But the written text is not—so to speak—a work in the *Teach Yourself Series*: it is the gymnastic instructor's handbook—the manual of direction for the spiritual guide who 'gives' the Exercises to him who performs them. The individual performing the Exercises not only need not but, in the early days before the text was available publicly, did not and probably could not himself have access to it. This is a point of great importance. The Jesuits 'gave' the Exercises: they did not give them to be read. This was from the start, even the false starts—if the expression be permitted—at Alcalá and Salamanca, the technique of St Ignatius himself; and the Exercises not only formed the instrument by which he first achieved the conversion, and then assured the life-long co-operation, of his first companions who formed the original Society of Jesus, but they remained—some would perhaps prefer to say, eventually became—the main permanent spiritual inspiration in the Society in perpetuity. They were in a sense the systematised, de-mysticised quintessence of the process of Ignatius's own conversion and purposeful change of life, and they were intended to work a similar change in others. Conversion, and the consequent taking of new and appropriate resolutions for the future:

these are the simple, straight-forward evangelical purposes of the *Spiritual Exercises*. There is nothing in them, says an Anglican commentator, 'which goes beyond the simplest and most fundamental truths of the Gospel'.[1] Their remarkable efficacy, their undoubted power, proved many times over, to 'change' men permanently, sprang from the extraordinary way in which they combined, by the instinct of spiritual genius, the accumulated spiritual wisdom of the past Christian centuries with the direct lessons learned by the saint himself in his own, in so many ways exceptional, spiritual experiences. The *Exercises*, as eventually made use of by the Society of Jesus in its wide general apostolate, and especially the development of retreats, spelt the formation of a new high-powered spiritual weapon capable of being applied with almost explosive results to men at all levels of spiritual need. For the 'conversion' and consequent 'election' of a new manner of life by the exercitant might operate —so to say—anywhere along the line of spiritual advance. It might work a change from indifference to regular Christian life; or from regular but tepid Christian life to a new purposeful fervour; or from fervour in the lay state to the embracing of the regular life in some religious order; or, indeed, again, from a normal regular observance within a religious order to a higher pitch of fervour and determination. The Exercises were—or at any rate soon became in the hands of experienced directors— infinitely flexible, capable of being modified according to the patient's character, or intellectual capacity, or his social condition of life, or the diagnosis of his inward condition by the discretion of the spiritual doctor. The medicine could be given in larger or smaller, in stronger or weaker, doses as required. But it was a medicine containing, like Alice's, so many good things that some mixture or other of it was always applicable. Here indeed was a weapon of unprecedented power: St Ignatius himself in tabloid form.

I do not think that this is the language of exaggeration. The

[1] W. H. Longridge (ed.), *The Spiritual Exercises of Saint Ignatius of Loyola, translated from the Spanish with a commentary and a translation of the* Directorium in Exercitia (London, 1930; 1st ed. 1919), p. xxxiv.

pastoral efficiency of the Jesuits has had an enormously wide range and has comprised a great variety of approaches. But the principles arising out of the *Exercises* have underlain all. Though there are some obscurities in the early story, I think myself that the history of St Ignatius and of the early society does in fact point to the central importance of the Exercises from the start both for the spiritual formation of the Jesuits themselves—at any rate in Italy—and for their influence on others.[1] Recent Jesuit work, especially that of Padre Iparraguirre,[2] strengthens the evidence for this. It was not only that frequently through the Exercises, as was perhaps their original historical purpose, men became Jesuits: some, like Nadal—whose name despite his very great importance never gets into the textbooks—only at long last after refusing the ordeal for many years.[3] But men in all walks of life, in high and low places, laymen and ecclesiastics, were found amenable to them; and many not only found their own lives changed permanently but became themselves thenceforward, sometimes from doubters, enthusiastic supporters of the society. Such, for example, were Contarini, Tolomeo Gallio, Ortiz, three men of high influence in Rome, to whom the society owed much in the facilitation of its recognition by Paul III in 1540, in circumstances of considerable difficulty and delicacy.

In analysing what the Exercises demand and involve, two elements can be picked out as central: first, the examination of conscience, which is stressed most of all at the beginning; and secondly, the method of meditation and the practical fruits to be culled from it, which runs throughout the whole and forms the core of the method. The systematic examination of conscience is done in two forms, first, the general examination and then the particular examination; this is a special and continuous technique,

---

[1] The opposite view was maintained by Bremond, *Histoire littéraire du sentiment religieux*, VIII (1928), 185 f., where he argued for a 'réaction ascéticiste' and a 'crise des Exercices' around 1580; note the attack on Watrigant, pp. 186, 229, and cf. J. de Guibert, *La spiritualité de la Compagnie de Jésus* (Rome, 1953), p. 3.

[2] I. Iparraguirre, *Historia de la práctica de los Ejercicios espirituales de San Ignacio de Loyola*: I, *Práctica de los Ejercicios... en vida de su autor (1522–56)* (Bilbao/ Rome, 1946), with fine bibliography.

[3] See M. Nicolau, *Jerónimo Nadal (1507–80), sus obras y doctrinas espirituales* (Madrid, 1949).

to be continued as long as necessary, in which the attack on special besetting sins is remorselessly pursued. It is interesting to compare the energy, vitality and pithiness of this famous technique of the particular examination—examining oneself two or three times daily—with the somewhat cumbrous recommendations characteristic of the medieval manuals for penitents. Here St Ignatius is concerned not so much with the classification of sins, for use in the confessional, but with the psychology of eradicating them. In the Ignatian meditations the whole developing tradition of the fifteenth-century teachers comes to a powerful climax. Meditation is not just a vague devotional 'thinking about' some biblical scene or religious consideration. It is the systematic concentration upon it of the whole attention of the mind. A certain preparation is each time necessary, with preludes in the form of prayers and recollection of purpose. Then comes the formation of the mental picture, followed by the application of the senses, the affections, and the will, point by point; and, finally, what St Ignatius calls the colloquy—the free prayer in converse with God, after the meditation proper, as each individual finds it comes to him to do, in order to concentrate and harvest the result in the taking of some definite determination. Every effort, in effect, must be made to bring every detail of an imagined scene vividly to one's mind, as if one were present, and then to draw fruit and grace in prayer and new resolutions. No stylised presentation, for example, of the Passion but the stark realities are to be imagined, with each sense.

The four weeks into which the *Spiritual Exercises* are divided are fixed and equal periods only by courtesy, like the days of creation. Each 'week' represents a stage—a true week being the optimum duration. But each week can be prolonged or shortened, and some of them even omitted, according to the decision of the director. The first week, purgative in nature, deals with the examination of conscience, confession and eradication of faults, the start of the struggle against self: the meditations concern sin and hell; and in this first week a preliminary election or choice of God, as against sin, is in fact tacitly made. But it is the second week that brings the climax of the specific election, or choice, with the famous opening meditations on the kingdom of Christ and the choice of standards, followed, before the election itself, by a series of meditations on the main events of our Lord's life from the Nativity to Palm Sunday. The election itself is a determination not merely to avoid sin—that has already been done in the first week—but actively to promote the kingdom of Christ in the state of life to which one is called, or to which one now decides that the call comes. The third week, illuminative we may say, following the traditional threefold conception of the stages of spiritual advance, strengthens the resolves already taken by a series of further meditations, mainly on the Passion. The fourth week, unitive in spirit, is based on meditations on the risen Lord, his glory, his love, which we are called upon to share. The complete series of meditations, after the preliminary ones in the first week on sin and hell and the opening one of the second week on the kingdom of Christ, cover the gospel story from the Nativity to the Resurrection; it has often been commented upon that neither here nor in the appended list of supplementary meditations is the divine history carried on further to the Ascension or to Pentecost.

In addition to the four groups of meditations proper, each with its accompanying outcome of personal resolve, the text of the *Exercises* contains in pithy, carefully phrased terms a number of other elements upon which the director can draw from time to time to assist his exercitant as may seem advisable, according to his character, his progress or his lack of progress, or the exact number of 'weeks' which are being undertaken. For it is possible—and indeed common—to do the Exercises only in part, though the election at the end of the second week is usually vital. The list of these other elements is quite long. First, the twenty annotations, or rules for the director, which open the text; secondly, the famous section known as the Principle or Foundation, a short but masterly summary of the end of man, his proper use of created beings, and his attainment of indifference to worldly conditions. This is placed at the beginning of the first week and is a nodal point in the whole scheme. Then there are special considerations to be made use of, to be brought to the notice of the exercitant, during the crucial second week, on different states of life, different classes of men, different degrees of humility. Then, coming after the end of the fourth week's meditations and fruits to be garnered, are, first, an additional series of mysteries of the life of our Lord, divided into points for meditation according to the plan of the four weeks; then twenty 'rules for the discernment of spirits', that is, tests for the genuineness of religious claims or emotions, again according to the way in which they may be useful during the experiences of the weeks; four rules for the distribution of alms; six observations concerning scruples; the famous eighteen rules for 'Thinking with the Church'—safeguards, that is, of orthodoxy—and lastly seventeen additional notes applicable to various points throughout the text. This curious literary form, in which the main expositions of the meditations and fruits to be sought in the four weeks are accompanied and followed up by a rich variety of running comments, as it were, in the way of rules for guidance, observations, considerations, analyses and so forth, shows clearly the nature of the whole; that it is designed for the director giving the Exercises, and not as a continuous text to be read by the exercitant. And, as if all this were not enough to ensure sufficient guidance and flexibility, there came into existence, first drawn up by St Ignatius and perfected later in the century under Acquaviva (1581–1615), forty further chapters of detailed advice to givers of the Exercises, known as the *Directory*.[1] Flexibility, indeed, was to be the main concern of the giver, who was to adapt the technique and the general plan to the particular needs, state, psychology, character, intelligence, stamina, of each individual concerned, without, however, altering the actual method of making what meditations were included: the composition of the mental scene, the application of the senses, the subsequent prayer and resolution. This recognition of the separateness and difference of each individual person is surely

---

[1] I. Iparraguirre (ed.), *Directoria exercitiorum spiritualium, 1540–99* (Monumenta historica Societatis Jesu: Monumenta Ignatiana, series II, nova editio, vol. II, Rome, 1955): a new edition of the relevant part of the next reference.

a high tribute to the perceptive humanity of St Ignatius. It runs
not only through the *Exercises*, but also, despite the stress on
implicit obedience, in the constitutions of his society as well.

Those who wish for a closer acquaintance with the *Exercises*
may be referred, from among a multitude of works, to the
definitive edition of the text—or more accurately, the texts—
made by the Spanish editors of the *Monumenta Historica Societatis
Jesu*,[1] to the various, and all masterly, recent works of Père de la
Boullaye, S.J.,[2] and to the useful and understanding English edition by the late Rev. W. H. Longridge of the Anglican Society
of St John the Evangelist.[3] Here, I pass on to ask how it was
that St Ignatius came to contrive this instrument, this finely
adaptable spiritual mangle, through which men were passed to
be brought out new.

Much has been written and continues to be written on the
history of the *Exercises* and the problem of their genesis and
sources. It seems clear that in the main they originate from and
are in fact a synthesised, as it were dehydrated, form of at least
parts of St Ignatius's own experiences of conversion and subsequent development, from the first conversion on his sick-bed,
through the formative stages of the pilgrimage to Montserrat,
the vital experiences of Manresa, the pilgrimage to Jerusalem, the
subsequent periods at Barcelona, Alcalá and Salamanca, right
up, indeed, to the important time at Paris. The main substance
of the *Exercises*, with practically all the most important elements
and meditations, would seem to date from the end of the time
at Manresa—1522–3. Some first retouches were no doubt made
in the experimental period when, as a student at Barcelona,
Alcalá and Salamanca, St Ignatius began to attract and teach
followers and was obliged to submit his text to the Inquisitorial
authorities. In this period, 1524–8, or perhaps even later, at
Paris, the important section known as the Principle or Foundation
was probably added. Then at Paris, where St Ignatius first

---

[1] *Exercitia spiritualia Sancti Ignatii de Loyola et eorum directoria* (Monumenta
Ignatiana, series II, Madrid, 1919).
[2] H. Pinard de la Boullaye, *Saint Ignace de Loyola, directeur d'âmes* (Paris, 1947);
*La spiritualité ignatienne: textes choisis et présentés par H.P.* (Paris, 1949); *Les
étapes de rédaction des Exercices de S. Ignace* (Paris, 1950). None of these works
is in the British Museum. [3] See above, p. 46 n.

began seriously to study philosophy and theology, and to attract as his disciples men who were also students, the *Exercises* seem to have undergone general revision. Various additions and annotations were added which show traces of the new intellectual environment, of an awareness of scholasticism, and of the wider ranges of human types who now came into the saint's purview; possibly also, for the first time, of an awareness of Protestantism. It was at Paris, apparently, that the famous rules for orthodoxy were formulated, also the well-known sections on the degrees of humility and on the three classes of men. At Paris, too, there seems to have been a recasting of the rules for the discernment of spirits—so important in an age of novelties and uncertainties and new claims—and a certain revision of the central point of the election, or choice of a state of life.

While, therefore, the main substance and structure of the *Exercises* were firmly laid down at a very early stage after, or even during, the experiences at Manresa—there are those who cull some satisfaction from reflecting that they may well have been written in a cell in the Dominican priory there!—they nevertheless underwent expansion and adaptation during the next dozen years or so until reaching their final form. I follow here Père Pinard de la Boullaye's brilliant little book *Les étapes de rédaction des Exercices de S. Ignace*[1] which, together with Padre Leturia's similar conclusions, would seem definitive. Behind this question, however, there lies a further important issue. How much did the teaching and influence of St Ignatius derive directly and independently from his own extraordinary experiences, mainly those undergone at Manresa in 1522–3, and how much from the spiritual traditions which surrounded him on all sides: the spiritual literature then influential in Spain, and Paris, the various external influences which came upon him in the course of his evolution—in a word, the whole historical, literary and spiritual atmosphere of the day which his *Exercises*, their method, spirit and purpose, seem to have caught up and so

[1] See above, p. 51, n. 2; P. Leturia, 'Génesis de los ejercicios de San Ignacio y su influjo en la fundación de la Compañía de Jesús (1521-40)', *Archivum historicum Societatis Jesu*, x (1941), 16–59, repr. in Leturia, *Estudios ignacianos*, ed. and rev. I. Iparraguirre (2 vols., Rome, 1957), II, 3–55.

brilliantly synthesised and focused? There is indeed a sense in which St Ignatius may be seen as the St Paul of the Counter-Reformation, and the problem of his influence upon it as similar to the analogous Pauline problem. Here was a man subject to a more or less sudden conversion, to special privileged illuminations (no historian, I think, could wholly discount Ignatius's own story of an extraordinary illumination on the banks of the River Cardoner at Manresa—to mention no other incidents), and destined to give new definition, impetus and modernity to the religious movement with which he was associated, and to carry it far and wide across the earth. Yet, on the other hand, as those of his followers are not slow to claim who emphasise most strongly the extent of his dependence on God's own direct private dealings with him, St Ignatius in no wise invented a new religion—any more, shall we say, than did St Paul?—and his spirituality, though conveyed through the *Exercises* in a practical technique that was brilliantly new and brilliantly successful, was nevertheless in full accord, when properly seen, with the dominant Catholic tendencies of his day and therefore drew undeniably upon a legacy from predecessors.

There is first of all a purely literary problem. Can any direct literary dependence on earlier texts be detected in the *Exercises*? In 1919 the able Spanish Jesuits who edited the texts of the *Exercises* in the *Monumenta Historica*[1] went very fully into this question in their introduction, referring learnedly to a large preceding literature. They concluded that no direct borrowing of phrases could be traced from the three books which so much influenced Ignatius in his earliest stages of conversion: the *Flos Sanctorum* (or Golden Legend), the *Vita Christi* of Ludolph the Carthusian, the *Imitation of Christ*, though they conceded that the author must have made considerable use of the multitudinous notes that he is known to have made on these works. In regard to a possible influence of Abbot Cisneros's *Ejercitatorio de la Vida Espiritual*,[2] which may have become known to St Ignatius during his short time at Montserrat, they concluded that here too there is no single instance of textual reproduction. In the actual

---

[1] See above, p. 51, n. 1.     [2] See above, p. 35, n. 2.

*Exercises* themselves, as distinct from the various additions, they admit only seven or eight passages of real resemblance, all of which, however, are passages that might just as well derive from Ludolph or à Kempis. Furthermore, they point out, and the point has cogency, that the form and object of the *Exercises* is quite different from that of the *Ejercitatorio*. The latter is a work for the general deepening of the spiritual life of monks; it is based upon, and assumes, the monastic horarium of liturgical prayer throughout the year. The Exercises, on the other hand, are, as we have seen, a special 'occasional' technique aimed primarily at effecting a change of life and possibly also a change of state of life. Commentators who have tried to find direct literary sources for the *Exercises* in a number of various quarters—the works of St Bernard, St Anselm, Gerard of Zutphen, Raymond Lull, Abbot Werner, Savonarola, Jan Mombaer, even Erasmus's *Enchiridion*—are similarly dealt with by the editors of the *Monumenta*. Possible parallels and resemblances turn out to be largely on points which, however important, are in fact commonplaces that might have one or more of any number of various inspirations; the textual similarities are never so close as to be completely convincing; moreover, St Ignatius could not, at the early time of the first writing of the *Exercises*, have read at all widely in patristic and medieval spiritual literature. He was still for all practical purposes a layman—and his early movement of apostolate, a lay one.

The findings of these editors in regard to direct literary dependence, though expressed in terms of perhaps undue asperity, are to my mind, on the whole, convincing, and would seem to have been very generally accepted. From a literary point of view, the *Exercises* are not just a patchwork from earlier writers—they are as original in expression as in general concept and design. And yet this is not the end of the problem. It is only the beginning of another, more difficult one. Granted that in detailed form, in elaboration of technique, in clarity and unity of purpose, the Ignatian *Exercises* are *sui generis*, different somehow from all the 'Exercises' and 'Scalae' and didactic treatises on meditation of the previous hundred and fifty years—in that everything in

## The Spirit of the Counter-Reformation

them is drawn up, as it were, in masterly battle-array under a skilled commander—yet it remains that their author lived in a certain historical setting; that he was part and parcel of an age; and that the expression of his perhaps unique spiritual gifts and perceptions and wisdoms was necessarily in the mode of his time. For all his uncovenanted privileges of special insight and understanding, which I for one would certainly not wish to question, St Ignatius was not, and could not be, a stained-glass figure abstracted from his environment and its influences. In recent decades, in fact, the history of St Ignatius, of his personal evolution and of his work has been much illuminated—not to say modernised—by able Jesuit scholars such as Padre Leturia, Père Pinard de la Boullaye, Père Watrigant, Père de Grandmaison, Père Dudon,[1] and others, who have understood and met this problem of envisaging St Ignatius in his historical setting, and who have had the enormous volume of materials in the *Monumenta Historica Societatis Jesu*, first published in Madrid, now being continued from Rome, from which to quarry. If so many critics have thought to find the 'origin' of various of the main ideas of the *Exercises* in previous writers it is because these ideas, however acquired by St Ignatius, are not in themselves, intrinsically and separately, new. Take the meditation on the kingdom of Christ, the famous choice of standards and the resolve to follow the standard of Christ rather than of his enemy—dramatic opening and climax, as it were, of the second week of the *Exercises*; all this is not just the colourful imagery of an old soldier turned evangelist, it is an age-old traditional concept of the spiritual writers, closely paralleled indeed in so un-Ignatian a book as Erasmus's *Enchiridion Militis Christiani*: paralleled there so closely that even Jesuits like Padre Leturia, Père Watrigant, and Père de Grandmaison will not follow the editors of the *Monumenta* in ruling it out utterly as a possible direct influence—whether Ignatius actually finished reading this work of Erasmus or no![2]

---

[1] See above, pp. 51, n. 2, 52 n., 32 n.; P. Dudon, *Saint Ignace de Loyola* (Paris, 1934). I do not know which work of Père de Grandmaison is referred to.

[2] Leturia, on page 23 of his article cited on p. 52 n., refers the matter to Watrigant, *La méditation fondamentale avant S. Ignace* (Enghien, 1907), p. 71, and R. García Villoslada, 'San Ignacio de Loyola y Erasmo de Rotterdam', *Estudios*

And indeed what else, at bottom, is the concept of the choice of standards than the classic one of the two allegiances, two communities, two cities—of the righteous and unrighteous—of God and the devil—Babylon and Jerusalem—what you will—which we find not only in St Augustine but in a host of other writers. Similarly, precedents can be found in plenty for the Ignatian doctrine of the three powers of the soul—memory, understanding, will; for some points in the method of meditation, of imagining ourselves actually present with each sense in turn at the scenes of our Lord's life and passion (made easier in St Ignatius's own case by his having actually visited Jerusalem); for the whole question of spiritual discernment, as well as for other less central points such as the regulation of the appetite in eating and drinking, the use of sleep etc. The *Exercises*, in fact, are at one and the same time uniquely new as a whole and in their method of activating men—but full of traditional spirituality in their particular points. The old wine in a new bottle—and brought to a new ferment. How did this come about? How did St Ignatius receive this deep understanding, practical wisdom, and succinct expressive power on paper, before he was either a wide reader of spiritual books or a scholar in the universities? Was it *all* infused at Manresa? Or did St Ignatius in fact undergo something which we could in the normal sense call a 'spiritual formation' at the hands of men?

That before his wound and conversion in 1521 Ignatius, though not an enthusiast in religious matters, had had close contact with them would seem evident from the fact that he was originally destined by his family for the Church, and indeed was a tonsured cleric of the diocese of Pamplona from early years. But it would appear that he must have turned away to the pursuit of the knightly and courtly life, with all its romantic self-indulgences; that he had made a deliberate 'election' of a state of life, as it were, but one turning away from God's service to that of an earthly prince. If this be so, there must always have been the

*eclesiásticos*, XVI (1942), 244–8. Gonzáles de Cámara says that humanist friends at Alcalá suggested that Ignatius should read it, and that he refused; Ribadeneira, that it was at Barcelona, and that he read but did not finish it because it 'lui faisait perdre sa dévotion' (Guibert, *Spiritualité de la Compagnie de Jésus*, p. 155).

recollection of it at the bottom of his mind. As a young page and then a knight at Tordesillas and at Arévalo contrasting examples of sin and piety would come his way plentifully: the easy relations of sensual people on the one hand; the atmosphere of official court piety on the other. On one side, duels, women, gaming; on the other, the ideals of chivalry, devotion, obedience, discipline in the service of a Lord. Doubtless Ignatius was no better than he should have been. But Arévalo was at this time one of the centres of the reviving Franciscanism in Spain so much promoted by Cardinal Jiménez de Cisneros. The influence of the Franciscan Ambrosio Montesino, whose translation of Ludolph's *Vita Christi* Ignatius later read on his sick-bed, was at work at Arévalo, where Ignatius may well have read his *Itinerario de la Cruz* dedicated to the Duchess of Nájera, wife of Ignatius's patron. There is reason, too, to suppose that he read at this time the *Triunfo de los Apóstoles* by the Franciscan poet Juan de Padilla, with its references to the Charterhouse of Seville, to which (and not to the nearer Charterhouse of Miraflores at Burgos) the saint at a later time once expressed a wish to retire. Add to all this early impressions of piety derived from the family circle, and it is clear that from a spiritual point of view Ignatius could not have been a complete *tabula rasa* when, on his sick-bed after Pamplona, the romances gave out and he was fain to turn to Montesino's translation of Ludolph and the lives of the saints. But at this period of what we may call his first 'conversion' these books of Germanic piety seem to have been the only religious books that he had by him and which inspired or at least accompanied his change of life. Under their aegis Ignatius made a new 'election'; the resolve to change his state of life from a knight of the world to that of a knight of Christ; to become a humble, poorly clad, penniless pilgrim. And it was as a preparation for a pilgrimage to Jerusalem, to set his eyes upon the exact sites of our Lord's life and sufferings, that he set out, when healed, across the north of Spain for the famous pilgrimage-shrine of our Lady of Montserrat, there to do vigil before the Madonna, to take, as it were, his new vows, and to exchange the rich garb of a knight for the coarse sackcloth of a pilgrim.

What really happened to Ignatius at Montserrat? It would be most interesting to know for certain! Was it simply a matter of three days of high generous religious emotion, marked by the—dare one suggest it?—slight exhibitionism of the famous vigil and discarding of knightly costume as well as by the more searching ordeal of a three days' general Confession? Or did St Ignatius at Montserrat, through his confessor the French monk Dom Chanones, come into touch, unexpectedly, with a powerful force of organised spirituality that was to supply him with the groundwork of something the need for which he had not previously understood but which he now saw that he must acquire—a solid spiritual formation at the hands of experienced guides? That this is in fact what occurred is the broad thesis of Dom Anselmo Albareda's extremely ingenious book *Sant Ignasi a Montserrat* (written, regrettably, in Catalan).[1] Dom Albareda, a monk of Montserrat, now librarian at the Vatican Library, maintains that it was this realisation of the need of formation which deflected Ignatius from his original purpose of proceeding immediately to Jerusalem (not any question of practical difficulties—plague in Barcelona, robbers on the road) and which sent him instead into unpremeditated retirement at the neighbouring town of Manresa where the Hospice of Santa Lucía could house him. Furthermore, Dom Albareda maintains that Ignatius did not stay merely three days on the holy mountain but that he lived there for some weeks as a penitent in a cave higher up than the monastery, receiving alms and spiritual advice; and that even when he finally betook himself to Manresa he came back frequently for conferences with Dom Chanones and others. This whole thesis has been severely criticised on every point by Jesuit authors, and I must confess that it seems to me very difficult to maintain in its entirety. The theory of the prolonged stay on the mountain and the frequent revisits rests only on the traditions of the monastery, and on late and circumstantial evidence, some of it hearsay and given by very old men at the beatification enquiries in the 1590s; moreover—and this seems to me extremely significant—St Ignatius himself gives no ground

[1] Monestir de Montserrat, 1935.

for it in the autobiography of his spiritual evolution which in his later years he dictated to Father Luis Cámara.[1] It is admitted on all hands that the claims of some seventeenth-century and even of certain more modern Benedictine writers, who maintained that St Ignatius owed everything to the Benedictines and that the *Exercises* flow directly from Abbot Cisneros's *Ejercitatorio*, cannot possibly be maintained; that such an extreme thesis is riddled with major misconceptions and critical impossibilities. Yet, despite the difficulties in maintaining Dom Albareda's less drastic thesis to the full, it seems to me nonetheless highly probable that Montserrat may have been a real turning-point and a step forward in the saint's spiritual evolution, bringing him into contact with a new force in organised religion and the realisation of how much he had to learn. It is highly plausible, to my mind, to suggest that this realisation turned him aside from the project of an immediate pilgrimage to Jerusalem, in order to retire, for the purpose of an intenser spiritual cultivation now seen to be necessary, to Manresa nearby. The possibility of this having happened, it seems to me, is underestimated by Dom Albareda's critics. Later relations of St Ignatius and the Jesuits with Benedictines were always especially cordial, so much so as even to suggest some kind of acknowledged debt.

But then what happened at Manresa? Normal formative influences were no doubt present—and, on his own admission, sought by the saint: the local Dominicans where he lodged for a time, a nearby Cistercian, certain pious women; he does not in his spiritual autobiography mention Montserrat or the Benedictines again. But all these now become secondary: indeed he records in his spiritual autobiography that no one could now give him any help in the extraordinary crisis of experiences which came upon him and out of which he emerged a new man (not this time by his own but by God's election) rich with mystical knowledge of God, mature in spirit after passing in a few weeks through a whole gamut of spiritual experiences which with others have been the spun-out story of a lifetime. It was now that he

[1] Leturia, '¿Hizo San Ignacio en Montserrat o en Manresa vida solitaria?', in *Estudios ignacianos*, I, 113–78, especially 175–8.

first read the *Imitation of Christ*, which he declared made every other spiritual work seem superfluous; now that he put down on paper the main points of the *Exercises*, before, the ordeals and enlightenments over, he set out, via Barcelona, for Jerusalem—now at last prepared for the deferred pilgrimage. Now he was, as it were, the mystic; illuminated, and in an interior sense changed and formed; but he was also the incipient apostle, beginning to sense that his call was not to the Carthusian cloister at Seville, nor to the reform of some lax order, not indeed to retirement, but to apostolic work for the greater glory of God and the good of souls; that, in a sense, he must hand on to others the fruits of the cleaning fires through which he had himself just passed. The Society of Jesus, not yet in his mind as such—not to take definite shape there for about another fifteen years or so—was nonetheless in principle conceived.

Jerusalem was a further climax; but one which served still further to clarify the future. His experiences in the Holy Land finally taught Ignatius that he was not destined to be an obscure hermit, either there or in his native land. With his return from Palestine there may be said to end the early ecstatic—mystic—stage of his religious evolution; the stage comparable with St Philip Neri's early quasi-Franciscan life in the catacombs and ruins of Rome, before he learnt that he must in the end give order and outward respectability to his way of life. The emotions and the will were now in harness. There remained the intellect. Education was required for the coming apostolate to be fruitful. Now well over thirty years old, Ignatius sat with mocking boys on hard benches in the lecture rooms at Barcelona, Alcalá and Salamanca successively, acquiring the rudiments of Latin. But always the pull was in two ways: to study, the immediate necessity; to the apostolate, the long-term basic urge. Early disciples gathered around; the Exercises began to be given, the Inquisition to be aroused. Was this strange errant cleric without Holy Orders an impostor? Another *alumbrado*, claiming direct light and ready to ignore the authorities of the Church—in contact perhaps with suspect circles? The Inquisitors saw that he was not; but they declared that he must not guide souls nor teach the difference between mortal and venial sin without further study. No doubt a sensible and salutary decision; one, certainly, which contributed to the saint's decision to leave Spain and go straight to the recognised fountain-head of traditional European scholastic learning, whither so many Spaniards had preceded him. In 1528 he was in Paris.

The effect upon St Ignatius of his years in Paris was profound. Here, in more ways than one, his whole outlook was widened and made more practical. A growing scholasticism of action, if we may use the phrase, accompanied the studies of scholastic philosophy and theology. A deeper sense of prudence and caution, of the practical, made themselves manifest, both in his dealings with men and in the additions and modifications to the *Exercises* which he now made, no doubt with new types of convert in mind. It was in Paris too that, if ever, he came into direct touch with the influence of the *devotio moderna*, for the whole religious atmosphere of the Collège de Montaigu at which he spent his first year had been formed by Mombaer and Standonck, and many monastic and other reforms had been attempted in Paris by representatives of the religious fervour from the Low Countries. Other influences in plenty, of course, were at work in Paris: spiritual, intellectual and humanist; the new biblical ardour of a Lefèvre as well as the strong conservatism of a Noël Beda. Paris was a centre of powerful forces and ideas such as Ignatius had not known before. Did all this pass him by in his campaign of choosing new disciples for his future work from among his fellow university students? Did he become here more aware of Protestantism and events in Germany and Switzerland? It can hardly have been otherwise. The vows on Montmartre—nearly contemporary with the *placards*—mark a further step in the evolution towards the foundation of the Society of Jesus. Ignatius is becoming a churchman as well as an apostle; the practical common sense, the genius for reality, the matter-of-factness of the future society are rising upon the basic spiritual foundations. If the nine—drawn from several nations—cannot visit Jerusalem together, they will put themselves at once at the disposition of the Pope. Six years more, after mission work in Italy, and the frustration of a joint pilgrimage to Jerusalem, would see the society established in Rome.

How insufficient, in view of all this history, it is to regard St Ignatius as simply an ardent Spaniard who brought medieval ideals of chivalry and a military outlook into his band of followers! The word *compañía* has no more necessarily military connotation than when applied in the Italian ten years earlier to St Angela's first group of pious lady-helpers. Translated into Latin, it is *societas*, not, for example, *cohors*.[1] In fact, St Ignatius and his Society of Jesus are the richest amalgams, formed by the successive influences which operated upon him in Spain, France and Italy, as well as being based upon his personal sanctity and the secrets of his direct knowledge of God.

The problem of the forces acting upon the origins of the society is in one aspect only part of a larger problem—that of foreign religious influences in the Spain of the early sixteenth century. The notion of a spiritually and intellectually isolated Spain at this period is a misconception formed by the casting-back of later views of Spain as a land impermeable to foreign influences. The new Spain of 1450 to 1550, which was so closely related, politically, to Italy, and subsequently to the Netherlands and to England; which was creating for herself a new empire in strange lands beyond the Atlantic, and which bore within herself the rich strains of Arab and Jew, Castilian and Basque, Catalan and Aragonese, could hardly form a solid watertight cultural entity. Today, specialists are perhaps more concerned to vindicate Spanish originality, or at least to disentangle the different strands of influence. I have already spoken of the Dominican influences passing between Italy and Iberia; and of what Fr Beltrán de Heredia has called the Savonarolian invasion of Spain[2], indicated by both direct and circumstantial evidence; though in respect of the Dominicans one must remember at the same time that the

[1] Cf. the remarks to a similar effect in G. R. Elton, *Reformation Europe, 1517–1559* (London, 1963), p. 203; O. Chadwick, *The Reformation* (Pelican History of the Church, III, Harmondsworth, 1964), p. 259; A. Guillermou, *Saint Ignace de Loyola et la Compagnie de Jésus* (Coll. *Maîtres Spirituels*, Paris, 1960), p. 50.

[2] 'La invasión savonaroliana' is the title of the first chapter of the work cited above, p. 17, n. 2.

## The Spirit of the Counter-Reformation

Castilian Preachers, for all their traditional intellectual contacts with Italy and Paris, had never succumbed to the all-powerful nominalism of the fifteenth century, and that the rise of the Thomist school of San Esteban at Salamanca, clinched though it was by the work of Vitoria after his return from Paris, was nonetheless largely indigenous. While Boehmer in his books on Ignatius studied the possibility of German mystical influences having played, in the ultimate analysis, a prominent part in his formation,[1] Altamira contended that all Spanish counter-reformation mysticism could be regarded as an importation from Germany and the Netherlands at the time of the Reformation.[2] Similarly, while a German called Muller could write a book trying to show that Ignatius copied the form and structure of his society from the example of certain Moslem societies,[3] it could also be asserted by others that Spanish medieval mysticism was rooted in Moslem philosophy.[4] Whatever we may think of this from the purely spiritual point of view, it is surely not absurd from the intellectual or literary standpoint. When Moslem influence has been detected by Asín and others in even Dante,[5] can any branch of *Spanish* thought or literature claim, a priori, to be exempt? Thinking of Erasmus's wide popularity in Spain up to the suppression of his works there, a popularity wider than he ever had in Italy, and studied in so masterly a way in Bataillon's big book,[6] we remember that Erasmus is himself but one form of a Netherlandish influence coming south—an ex-Canon Regular of Windesheim; while any reader of the valuable and interesting work on Erasmus's early period by Paul Mestwerdt, a young German scholar killed in the first World War, will

---

[1] H. Boehmer, *Loyola und die deutsche Mystik* (Sächsischen Akademie der Wissenschaften, phil.-hist. Klasse, Bd. XXIII, Heft 1, Leipzig, 1921), p. 21, etc.

[2] I have not found the reference. In *Historia de España y de la civilización española*, III (3rd ed., Barcelona, 1913), 554, Altamira describes the mystics as being 'sí influídos por los alemanes contemporáneos [sic], diferentes de ellos por su ortodoxia y su repulsión a las extravagancias...'

[3] Herrmann (sic) Muller (presumably pseud.), *Les origines de la Compagnie de Jésus: Ignace et Lainez* (Paris, 1898).

[4] Altamira, *Historia de España*, I, (2nd ed., 1909), 570, à propos of Ramón Lull.

[5] M. Asín Palacios, *La escatología musulmana en la Divina Comedia* (Madrid, 1919): see U. Cosmo, *A handbook to Dante studies* (Oxford, 1950), p. 149.

[6] See above, p. 11 n.

not underestimate the influence of the *devotio moderna* upon him.[1]

More research needs to be done, perhaps, before the real nature and extent of Germanic influence on the sixteenth-century Spanish mystics can be adequately gauged; Groult's book on the subject is inconclusive[2] and I have not yet been able to see a recent general work on this point, by a Spanish Franciscan.[3] But it is noteworthy that the late Padre Crisógono, O.D.C., an outstanding Carmelite scholar who died all too young, wrote of St John of the Cross and Tauler that 'the history of mysticism knows of no two mystics who resemble one another more closely',[4] and very recently another Spanish Carmelite scholar has seen a probable literary influence on St John in Ruysbroeck. Professor Allison Peers, though not subscribing to all Padre Crisógono's views on St John, is nevertheless concerned to indicate adequately the foreign influences in Spanish mysticism—especially Tauler, Ruysbroeck and Gerson. But in estimating the real originality of St Teresa and St John, who quote so little from other writers, we are up against the same sort of problem as we are in regard to the originality of St Ignatius. Behind all three lie centuries of tradition, and influences both Latin and Germanic. All are creative in a real sense, in that they fashion out of their materials —their experiences and their literary sources—something new. But it is undeniable that Germanic mysticism, like the Germanic *devotio moderna* with its large contribution to the systematised meditation of the Ignatian Exercises, like, again, the Germanic devout humanism of an Erasmus, were among the many influences present in renaissance and counter-reformation Spain.

Let me here, in conclusion, enter this *caveat*. In suggesting the existence of similar problems of derivation or influences

[1] *Die Anfänge des Erasmus: Humanismus und 'Devotio Moderna'* (Leipzig, 1917).

[2] P. Groult, *Les mystiques des Pays-Bas et la littérature espagnole du seizieme siècle* (Louvain, 1927).

[3] J. Sanchís Alventosa, *La escuela mística alemana y sus relaciones con nuestros místicos del Siglo de Oro* (Madrid, 1946): no. 2005 of bibliography in E. Allison Peers, *Studies of the Spanish mystics*, III (London, 1960).

[4] Quoted, with dissent, by Allison Peers, *St John of the Cross and other lectures and addresses* (London, 1946), p. 41, from Crisógono de Jesús Sacramentado, *San Juan de la Cruz* (2 vols., Madrid, 1929), I, 51. I do not know who the 'other Carmelite scholar' is.

undergone, in respect of the Spanish mystics and of St Ignatius's *Exercises*, I must not be taken as implying that I equate the two. Mystic, in a real sense, St Ignatius himself undoubtedly was; favoured, at Manresa principally, and then again later in life while composing the constitutions of his society in 1544–5, with special illuminations, special understandings, special and no doubt lasting intimacies with God. But despite the comparisons which can be and have specifically been made, recently again by Padre Larrañaga, between Ignatius's experiences of 1544–5 as recorded in his *Spiritual Diary* and the autobiography and other works of St Teresa,[1] it is surely plain that it must be difficult, by and large, to fit St Ignatius's case into the normal 'main-line' framework of Catholic mysticism and the development of contemplative prayer as we see it in the Spanish Carmelites, St Teresa, St John of the Cross, and other sixteenth-century Spanish mystics. Moreover, however this may be, it remains the fact that the *Spiritual Exercises*, this recipe for conversion, written substantially at Manresa itself, is not a work of mysticism or contemplation in the technical sense—despite St Ignatius's employment of the word 'contemplation' to denote a certain mode of imaginative discursive meditation. Indeed, nothing is so astonishing as the outcome of the raptures and visions of Manresa in this very unmystical, almost matter-of-fact, technique of the *Spiritual Exercises*. There is, of course, nothing in the *Exercises* either to suggest or to discourage the idea of the converted man being able eventually to reach the attainment of contemplative prayer as Grace develops in him, a prayer rising above vocal utterances, mental images or discourse of reason; and there are those who have maintained that in the meditations of the fourth week there are direct preliminaries, if not invitations, to the contemplative state. The *Exercises*, remember, are not a general philosophy of prayer or the spiritual life as a whole. They are a way of conversion —usually a *première*, not Lallemant's *deuxième conversion*. But in fact, whether this happened according to the mind of St

---

[1] V. Larrañaga, *La espiritualidad de S. Ignacio comparada con la de S. Teresa de Jesús* (Madrid, 1944). Larrañaga is the author of the introduction to the *Obras completas de San Ignacio de Loyola* in the *Biblioteca de autores cristianos*, LXXXVI (Madrid, 1952). Neither of these is in the British Museum.

Ignatius or not, there developed in the society, especially under the generalships of Mercurian and Acquaviva, a view that contemplation proper was an inappropriate form of prayer for members of an institute whose life was devoted to activity.[1] There have, of course, been true Jesuit contemplatives in the normally accepted sense of the word—Balthasar de Álvarez, confessor of St Teresa (who was commanded, however, by Mercurian to return to the methods of the *Exercises*), Álvarez da Paz, Provincial of Peru, Lallemant and Surin in early seventeenth-century France, and others. Yet on the whole, in the society's own life and therefore also in its pastoral activities it has not promoted this higher way of prayer even in those who feel called to it—this prayer which doubtless St Ignatius knew and experienced, but which he did not deal with in the *Spiritual Exercises*. The mystic and the active man merged naturally in St Ignatius himself. They were not encouraged to do so in the society. What difficult theological problems in regard to Grace and the nature of prayer are involved herein, I cannot here discuss.

[1] Bremond, *Histoire littéraire*, VIII, 228 f.; J. de Guibert, 'Le généralat de Claude Aquaviva (1581–1615): sa place dans l'histoire de la spiritualité de la Compagnie de Jésus', *Archivum historicum Societatis Jesu*, X (1941), 59–93, and *La spiritualité de la Compagnie de Jésus*, pp. 219–270; Allison Peers, *Studies of the Spanish mystics*, III, 181.

# 4

## THE REORIENTATION OF THE RELIGIOUS LIFE[1]

The life of religious communities has always been so intimately bound up with the *bene esse* of Catholicism that their condition at any given historical moment is an almost infallible guide to the condition of the Church as a whole; while every successful movement of general reform within the traditional framework of Catholicism has invariably been accompanied, if not inspired, by reforms and progress in what is technically called the 'religious' life. It is indeed in full accord with the principles of Catholicism that there should be a spiritual correlation between the life of those who have 'abandoned the world' and of those who remain in it, for—while there are no doubt exceptions to this, both in respect of individuals, and perhaps of historical periods—the urge towards the following of the counsels of perfection in community life bound by vows does not spring primarily from despair of life or disappointment in the wicked world. The truest springs of monasticism should be seen in the desire for God rather than in the flight away from the world; and the spread of monasticism as a sign rather of the power of religion than of the decay of general morality.

At every crucial point in the middle ages, to go back no further, the historical link between western monasticism and religious reform (and not only religious reform but the whole development of society too) is evident. The Carolingian endeavour to reorganise western Europe had its monastic reflection in the work of St Benedict of Aniane. The Cluniac reform partners the

---

[1] The account given here may be compared with Evennett's article, 'The New Orders', in the *New Cambridge Modern History*, II. The bibliography which he prepared in conjunction with it will appear in due course, and may dispense with detailed references here. Three general works to which he draws particular attention are M. Heimbucher, *Die Orden und Kongregationen der katholischen Kirche* (2 vols., Paderborn, 1933–4); A. Cistellini, *Figure della riforma pretridentina* (Brescia, 1948); P. Schmitz, *Histoire de l'ordre de Saint Benoît*, III (Maredsous, 1948). See also above, p. 13, n. 5; p. 27, n. 4.

Hildebrandine movement; the Cistercians accompany the twelfth-century renaissance and culture. The crusades bred the crusading orders. Then, in the thirteenth century there arose the new ideal of the friar, set against the background of new economic and intellectual advances and the working out of the policies of Innocent III and his successors. Monks, friars, canons, crusading orders: here are the four main types of regular religious life offered to men in the last three centuries of the middle ages, in institutions which dug themselves into the fabric of society in their material as well as their spiritual aspects, in a manner which led to an evergrowing tension arising out of the paradoxical aspects of their duplex—rather than double—life.

Between the appearance of the thirteenth-century friars, together with their third orders for lay people, and the Counter-Reformation, no completely new form of corporate religious life made its appearance. The sole possible exception is offered by the Brethren of the Common Life, who in some ways, but some only, dimly foreshadow the counter-reformation congregations of reformed priests. The state of monasticism in this period, however, did not cease to mirror the general state of the Church, especially, it would seem, in the fifteenth century, that most mysterious of periods, full of the most colourful and glaring juxtapositions, a century indeed of wheat and tares *par excellence*, but in which the harvest appeared to be constantly receding. The problems involved in appraising later medieval monasticism are surely, in the last analysis, the same as those presented by late medieval Catholicism as a whole, for the symptoms are similar and spring from the same causes. There is great need of a well-documented, reflective study of western monasticism between say, 1400 and 1600, tracing the development of its ideals and its fortunes through the fifteenth century and the humanistic-dominated period, and through the Reformation and the Counter-Reformation, taking into account the whole range of factors—political, economic, intellectual, as well as spiritual—which played upon monasticism in both its theory and its practice. For such a study, could any one man attempt it, wide sympathies and wide historical views would need to be mated with thorough scholarship and an exact and orderly mind. Without wishing in any way to reflect upon the memory of one who was both an erudite scholar and an earnest seeker after truth,[1] I say advisedly that this book has not yet been written, and that a series of colourful lucky-dips into a bran-tub of somewhat arbitrarily selected sources does not form any substitute. For English monasticism, up to the dissolution, we can indeed justifiably expect in due course such a study as I have in mind,[2] but English monasticism in the 150 years before the dissolution, both for men and for women, seems to have moved in a secluded back-water, and with the exception of the introduction of the Observant Franciscans appears to have been singularly untouched by the various forces and manifestations of outward reform and inner renewal to be found on the continent in the fifteenth and early sixteenth centuries.

As was true of religious reform in general, so of monasticism in particular, the fifteenth century was indeed paved with good intentions. Its records are full of reforming movements, of spreading monastic enthusiasms, of canonised or beatified friars and nuns, of obvious spiritual power and widespread influence —for the most part, but not exclusively, in Italy. Every order of friars—not only the Franciscans, but also the Dominicans, Augustinians and Carmelites and Servites—had its reformed houses of observance, often organised into autonomous provinces and often attaining considerable numbers, in which the common life, enclosure, regularity, poverty, study were better observed than among the conventuals. The appearance, if only on a small scale, of new friar-like institutions, such as the Friars Minims, the Jeronimites, the Jesuates, showed that the creative powers of mendicancy were not yet wholly exhausted. In the monastic world proper, in the main line of Benedictinism, the many reformed houses, or new congregations, that sprang from San Benito at Valladolid, Santa Justina of Padua and Subiaco in Italy, Melk in Austria, Bursfeld in north Germany, Casel in

---

[1] G. G. Coulton, *Five centuries of religion* (4 vols., Cambridge, 1923–50).
[2] David Knowles, *The religious orders in England* (3 vols., Cambridge, 1950–9), especially vol. II (1955).

Bavaria, Chezal-Benoît in France, show numerous points of interest both constitutionally and spiritually, and in their time they flourished. But in the first decades of the sixteenth century it was agreed that the need for reform was almost as great as ever, and humanist literature did not allow this ever to be forgotten. Among the friars the observants were for long a minority among a much larger number of conventuals. Relations between the two were always difficult; and one can appreciate, as Luther's history illustrated, how the exact observance of the observants might be capable of appearing as a pharisaical literalism in the eyes of sensible and sincere conventuals.[1] But the difficulties facing reform by no means vanished when in course of time the Franciscans definitely split into two independent branches of observants and conventuals, before the Capuchin movement arose in the fullness of time as a new, more drastic, more successful version of primitive observance. Among the Dominicans, Augustinians, Carmelites and Servites, the supreme control of the order eventually passed into the hands of observant superiors. Despite ups-and-downs well exemplified, for example, in the case of the Augustinians, as set out in Professor Jedin's illuminating life of Seripando,[2] one gets the impression that the course of reform among the friars came much more near to an orderly pattern of continuous development than anything found among the Benedictines and their off-shoots, where the whole fifteenth- and early sixteenth-century pattern is much more diverse and disconnected.

Several reasons can be put forward for this. While there would seem to be more definite indications among the various Benedictine reforms than among the friars of a new and more intensive cultivation of the only real basis of permanent reform, a doctrine and practice of prayer taught systematically to the rising generation, yet the flail of commendams, by which abbeys were given to non-monastic superiors, fell constantly and heavily on the monastic houses, especially in France, but in Italy, Spain and Germany too, weakening them at the crucial point of ab-

[1] Cf. Aubenas and Ricard, *L'Eglise et la Renaissance*, p. 289.
[2] See above, p. 10, n. 2.

batial authority. The absence of central organisation, too, was not—at this period, at any rate—to the advantage of the Benedictines, and this was widely recognised in the constitutional structure of the new fifteenth-century federal congregations of abbeys, providing for regular congregational chapters and visitations (as indeed earlier papal legislation had required) and for a new practice of temporary in place of life abbots. So far did this go in the Paduan congregation that the monk there was professed for the congregation as a whole, not for any one specific house, and the temporary abbots were appointed by the central authorities at Santa Justina. Even German Bursfeld did not go so far as Italian Padua in this respect, nor, I think, did Spanish Valladolid. Austrian Melk, though a vital centre of reform, founded no new congregation. By the time of Luther, however, the first impetus seems to have more or less died out of all these Benedictine reforms, though one must not forget exceptions such as early sixteenth-century Montserrat or Chezal-Benoît. Benedictinism, in general, was tossing hither and thither in a general doldrum, about to face centuries of extinction in England and northern Germany and elsewhere. The end of Bursfeld is a tragic and pitiable story.[1]

But the more centralised organisation of the orders of friars, weakened though it was by the frequently anomalous position of the observant congregations within them, could not save them any more than the Benedictines, or indeed the closer-knit Cistercians, from disaster where the Reformation prevailed, or guarantee immediate and lasting reform where it did not. It was, indeed, from the friars and monks that a very high proportion of the early Protestant leaders and preachers came, and it was an added tragedy for all the orders that just when the friars were beginning to produce really outstanding generals—men like Cajetan among the Dominicans, Giles of Viterbo and Seripando among the Augustinians, Audet among the Carmelites, Laurerio and Bonucci among the Servites—they should find their efforts and authority more and more undermined by the continual stream of dispensations issued, often quite unbeknown to them,

[1] Schmitz, *Histoire de l'ordre de Saint Benoît*, III, 272-4.

to their subjects by Roman tribunals, chiefly the *signatura gratiae* and the penitentiary, by the organs, that is, of that very papal authority which at its highest level smiled benignly on their reforming efforts. Dispensations to hold property; to live without good reason outside their order: the *licentia standi extra*; to hold ordinary benefices; to be transferred to less severe orders—all this made systematic reform and precautions against new doctrine in the highest degree difficult. But so largely, in almost every part of medieval Catholic Europe, had the friars taken over the work of pastoral activity, in preaching, in the confessional, in indulgence proclamations and so forth; so securely were they supported in their immense privileges and exemptions from episcopal control by the Apostolic See, that the direst consequences must follow inevitably from their contamination by the new doctrines. The question of the reform of the orders of friars was thus not a secluded watertight one: it was of front-line importance in regard both to the general pastoral efficiency of the Church as a whole and to the spread of the new beliefs. If Benedictines, Carthusians, Canons Regular, Cistercians were part and parcel of society in an important material and economic way, the friars were even more deeply so from the pastoral point of view, and it was this which gave the question of their reform its enormous importance and prominence over that of the monastic orders proper. Here, certainly, is one undoubted case where the acute fear of Protestantism applied an agonising spur to a long-standing, long-labouring reform movement.

I am not primarily concerned here with the reforms of the older orders which, nevertheless, during the sixteenth and seventeenth centuries, showed, together with admitted failures, also surprising successes. Instead of the drastic proposals earlier entertained to let a number of them die out and to group the rest under three rules and organisations, the more sensible, practical reforms sketched at Trent in 1563 were taken as a basis. The history of the Capuchin Franciscans, overcoming their early setbacks, of the Spanish reformed Carmelites, of the Spanish Dominicans and of Benedictine congregations like those of Vannes and St Maur, show what outstanding contributions to pastoral

work, intellectual development, scholarship, and the understanding and promotion of mystical prayer the older orders
could still make. Of the Carthusians—the Charterhouse *nunquam
reformata quia nunquam deformata*—we can say that judging by
the lives and influence of numerous German Carthusians, in the
sixteenth as well as the fifteenth century, a larger interest and
practical usefulness in the external affairs of the Church were
manifest by them at this period than we are accustomed to
associate with modern Parkminster or Miraflores.

But it is rather with the newer forms of religious community
life which came into being to meet the direct challenges of the
sixteenth century that I am now concerned—those which are to
the Counter-Reformation what the Benedictines were to the
early middle ages and the friars to the thirteenth century. The
challenge of the new epoch was felt in two spheres, that of
spirituality and that of pastoral efficiency, and the two were not,
of course, in watertight compartments. The challenge was met
on both fronts, as it were, not only by the new type of seminary-
trained secular clergy, but also by the new congregations of clerks
—priests—regular or secular, of which the Society of Jesus was
from the first intrinsically the most significant and very soon
became the most influential example. The object of these was
not the salvation of their members in retirement from the world
and in the concentration on prayer and austerities. Abandoning
certain important aspects and practices of the monastic life as
lived hitherto, and to that extent deferring—perhaps unconsciously—to humanistic criticisms, though rigidly maintaining
the three traditional vows, these institutes set themselves up to
give a high example of the priestly life, lived in full honour and
decorum, and to devote themselves to pastoral activity. They
soon established themselves as an accepted, indeed as an almost
essential, constituent element within the Church, proliferating
in due course, and especially after the French Revolution, in the
very numerous congregations of men and women so prominent
in modern Catholicism.

The Society of Jesus was not the first, in time, of these new
institutes to be founded; but it was the one which carried the

ctivity and the reaction from medieval monasticism
was preceded by the Theatines, the Barnabites, the
-the latter so called after the place of their foundation.
ct, during the whole course of the twenty years before
the Bull *Regimini Militantis Ecclesiae* of 1540, the extraordinary
story of St Ignatius's life and activities on which I offered some
comments in my last lecture was prefiguring in all its stages the
form and spirit of the society, in a way which makes it not
impossible to see a mystical truth in the Jesuit tradition that this
form and spirit were divinely revealed to the saint at Manresa
in 1522, despite the undeniable fact that not until 1539 did the
finished plan of the society, or indeed the decision to found one,
emerge clearly formulated in his conscious mind. To give the
Jesuits priority of importance, however, we do not need to
appeal to this kind of consideration. Their rapid rise to prominence, the universal nature of their work, the quick perception
by contemporaries of their novelty—seen equally clearly, perhaps
more clearly, by those who opposed its foundation as by those
who aided it—the quite unique place which they won in the life
and work of Catholicism, even the opposition and dislike which
came to them, all these give ample warrant for taking them as
the type. They were not, as a well-known writer on the decline
and fall of the medieval papacy would have it, 'the last flowering
of western Monasticism'.[1] They were the sudden blossoming of
a new and very modern form of religious association appropriate
to the needs of the modern Catholic Church.

It is difficult for a modern Catholic to appreciate to the full
exactly how revolutionary—how modernist—the institute of the
Society of Jesus must have appeared in 1540. The abandonment
of the common recitation of the daily hours of the divine office
in choir, hitherto unquestionably accepted as an essential feature
of all communal priestly life, seemed to some contemporaries so
shocking as to be almost heretical. Twice, supreme papal authority
forced a temporary return to the practice, to the great embar-
rassment of the society. The point was in fact crucial to the

[1] L. Elliott Binns, *The history of the decline and fall of the mediaeval papacy* (London, 1934), p. 369, n. 30.

institute and had a direct bearing both on the very personal spirituality fostered by the society in its own members, and on its dedication, with equal emphasis, to the salvation and perfection of others. The new spirituality of the Jesuit priest was indeed intensely personal. Community prayers and long liturgical functions were reduced to a minimum. Action was prayer, and prayer led to action. Though the mystique of the society as a whole was doubtless strong—like the growing mystique of the state over against the individual—yet the sense of corporate, and of liturgical, worship, as the middle ages knew it and as twentieth-century Catholicism was to revive it, was deliberately thrust aside (without its own value in its own place being questioned) in order that opportunities should be sought along other more actively apostolic lines for the greater glory of God. This was no longer the monastic ideal, but something different. The traditional vows of chastity, poverty and obedience, essential for the personal spirituality and the apostolic labours of the society, were found capable of taking new institutional expressions, and the break with traditional monasticism was further seen in the abandonment of many monastic externals: a special dress, rituals in daily life and customs, and all compulsory asceticisms, which had become objects of derision in the eyes of humanist or heretical scoffers. *Cucullus non facit monachum. Monacatus non est pietas.* The followers of St Ignatius—despite the story of the saint's refusal to finish reading Erasmus's *Enchiridion Militis Christiani*—wore no distinctive dress, no religious habit; no more than did those other 'reformed priests', the Theatines, who nevertheless laid great stress on the communal performance of the choir offices. The Jesuits were definitely encouraged not to mortify their bodies to excess by fasting, self-scourging, or denial of sleep to the extent of harming their studies or their activities on behalf of others; mortification in the bodily sense was no longer a matter of common rule but one of allowable private enterprise strictly controlled, nevertheless, by a sensible and ever-observant authority.

The deliberate abandonment of many of the hitherto accepted features of monasticism may indeed in some ways have helped the society to win papal approval just at the most difficult moment for monasticism, three years after the *Consilium de Emendanda Ecclesia* of 1537, which had voiced the opinion of the extremists in Roman reforming circles who held that no further religious orders should be allowed and that the existing ones should be reduced to two or three main types of normality. Yet influential among the signatories to the *Consilium*—some would say the actual author of the document—was Carafa, well capable, as co-founder of the Theatines with St Cajetan, of distinguishing between a monastic religious order and a company of 'reformed priests', though traditional enough to insist that even 'reformed priests' should chant or sing the priestly canonical office in common. But neither Theatines nor Barnabites had so clear a perception as Ignatius and his companions of what the life of a community of reformed priests dedicated as much to the good of their neighbour as to the salvation of their own souls—seeing, indeed, the one almost entirely in the other—should be, or could be, in the modern world, using the new spiritual technique of private meditation, according to the example of the *Spiritual Exercises*, and finding prayer in work to offset the absence from their life of the long hours spent in communal or liturgical worship, as in the life of monk, canon or friar.[1]

This 'modernisation' of the communal priestly life, for the good of others, almost Erasmian in some particulars, runs through the life and spirit of the society. We should notice the extreme importance laid on study: the amount of space devoted in the constitutions of the society to the colleges for scholastics—young

[1] The text of the Jesuit Constitutions is in Monumenta historica Societatis Jesu: Monumenta Ignatiana, series iii, *Constitutiones*, vol. III (Rome, 1938); and *Obras completas de S. Ignacio de Loyola* (Madrid, 1952). The only complete English translation seems to be the anonymous one published London, 1838 (Iparraguirre, below, no. 438); English translations of the educational part (iv) of the Constitutions and of the *Ratio Studiorum*, in E. A. Fitzpatrick, *St. Ignatius and the Ratio Studiorum* (New York, 1933), and G. E. Ganss, *St. Ignatius' idea of a Jesuit university* (Milwaukee, 1954; 2nd ed. 1956); cf. A. P. Farrell, *The Jesuit code of liberal education* (Milwaukee, 1938). For bibliography consult I. Iparraguirre, *Orientaciones bibliográficas sobre S. Ignacio de Loyola* (Rome, 1957), and J.-F. Gilmont and P. Daman, *Bibliographie ignatienne* (Louvain, 1958). Both are excellent, especially the first, and go up to 1957; for subsequent work, see *Archivum historicum Societatis Jesu*. See Postscript, pp. 128–32.

Jesuits doing their studies; the care taken to suit the length and substance of the scholastic courses to the individual man; the ideals to be aimed at, the allowances to be made, even the temporary priority to be given by the scholastic to study over prolonged spiritual exercises. Why and how had St Ignatius in Barcelona, after his return from Jerusalem, suddenly resolved to have himself educated? What influence convinced him that, in a sense, pure spirituality was not enough for the task he had sensed himself to be called to of converting others? Not, surely, the influence of humanistic literature demanding a better educated clergy. Hardly, perhaps, because the great Cardinal Cisneros had founded the University of Alcalá—to which Ignatius himself went, after Barcelona—for this express purpose. Yet in effect Ignatius in the long run probably did more for the appropriate education of the clergy of the Roman Catholic Church than either Erasmus or Cisneros.

The training of the Jesuit faithfully reflects the life of the founder. The first two years of probation, with their initiation into the spirituality of the society, the performance of the Exercises, and with the six specific trials laid down for novices in the constitutions, reflect the ardent pilgrim of Montserrat, Manresa and Jerusalem, the first rapturous stage of the saint's pilgrim's progress. Then come the long years of study in the scholasticate, with their definite 'let-up', so to speak, in spiritual tension, giving a training in prudence, patience, self-control, toleration of the humdrumness of life; as St Ignatius steeled and trained himself in Paris in his long years of study—how uncongenial to him God alone knows, but recognised to be necessary—even while he was gathering round himself the eight with whom he made private vows in Montmartre on 15 August 1534, a few weeks before the affair of the *placards* and the probable weeks of Calvin's flight from France. Then, after the completion of studies, comes the third year of the Jesuit's special probation, the tertianship—finally organised under the generalship of Acquaviva (1581–1615)—which would seem to correspond to the years spent in Italy by Ignatius and his companions, after they had left Paris, in pastoral and missionary work in the north

Italian towns, where they made contacts with the Theatines and other centres of reform, before the foundation of the society in 1540 and the taking of their official vows in the following year. After the tertianship the Jesuit is finally professed in the society, in one or other rank, and ordained, as St Ignatius was in this Italian period.

The stress on education is perhaps the most surprising, the most unexpected thing in St Ignatius's surprising life, considering his origins and earliest history. Yet it is all-important and highly significant. If I call it both modern and humanistic I do not wish to be misunderstood. All the older orders, especially the friars, had provided for study in the training of their members. Insistence on adequate studies was a feature of all the attempted fifteenth-century reforms. Yet with the Jesuits it represented the new conviction of the new age, shared by all religious bodies not wholly fanatical, that only a properly and appropriately educated minister was really competent to do the pastoral work for which Christians were everywhere crying out. For St Ignatius this education should be not merely the university degree ·which in the middle ages was by itself a title to a benefice, but something integrated into and forming the completion of a course of spiritual probation. It is significant, too, that only on the completion of his studies was a Jesuit scholastic admitted into the real body of the society, either as a spiritual coadjutor or as a professed member. With the older orders profession in perpetual vows, irrevocable in theory, immediately followed one year's noviciate, and then studies began: the order was committed to its members and they to it before their suitability for higher education was tested. The Jesuit constitution was so arranged that while the scholastics were committed to the society by their vows already made, the society was not correspondingly committed to them, and they could be either dismissed or perhaps offered the status of lay brothers, if found unsuitable for the studies appropriate to the priesthood.

Education as conceived by the society was not, of course, in our modern sense, fully liberal. It was not the cultivation of the mind and the mind's faculties of independent individual thought, for the mind's own sake. It was not an intellectual search for truth without prepossessions, or a cultural search for form or beauty irrespective of moral considerations. While it accepted and borrowed much from contemporary humanism, using the classical authors for literary training and appreciation, it necessarily adhered to traditional methods in philosophy and theology, though not clinging to the *Sentences* of Peter Lombard as the sole main textbook, and developing an anxiety to interpret dogma and morals to the best advantage. And while the constitutions and the examination of would-be entrants to the society refer to the necessity for submission not only of will but also of opinions, where theological opinion is officially free, to those of the society as a whole, the technical training in thought and, in due course, in research made it possible for individual Jesuits to make original contributions to all branches of learning. If learning, within its own particular sphere, could be regarded as making for the greater glory of God, then it was a suitable pursuit for a Jesuit. But, in origin, the institution of the scholasticate and the provision for Jesuit universities, primarily for Jesuits themselves, made in the constitutions have behind them a pastoral motive and are based on the conviction that the best work for souls could only be done by men thoroughly and appropriately trained not only in pure spirituality but also in the various sacred sciences. Learning was approached as the handmaid of religion, with every care lest she become the corrupter of morals or the seducer of faith. No truth defined by the Church should be questioned. No conclusion of the intelligence incompatible with the Church's defined dogma could be entertained. The Church's orders concerning the use of biblical texts and biblical studies in general must be obeyed. Disobedience in these spheres must be punished. It is anachronistic to suppose that any sixteenth-century Jesuit could have had the reactions of a twentieth-century Englishman to the principles and practices of index and Inquisition.

Freedom from a monastic routine, however, was a mark of Jesuit life that made eventually for versatility and a development of a rich variety of labours and undertakings such as never occurred in the history, for example, of the Theatines. All details of horarium were matters for local regulation according to local conditions and requirements. Life in a novitiate house would be one thing; in a scholasticate, another; in a professed house, different again. In India, Brazil or Japan, different yet again; and mission work of this sort was always a high priority. Humane and sensible provisions in regard to the preservation of health, prudent considerations in respect of what is due in the world in general to rank, birth and authority, jostle in the constitutions with the reiterated rule that not a penny must ever be taken in return for any spiritual or educational work. Nor must the spiritual direction of nuns be undertaken. The society, in all its prudence, must utterly shun all avenues leading to that venality and scandal which all recognised as deadly poisons running throughout the Church's veins. Again we are struck by the extraordinary mingling of enthusiastic idealism and practical prudence in the society, deriving from the character of its founder.

I have tried to stress what I consider to have been in the days of its origin the modern as opposed to the medieval characteristics of the Society of Jesus, the various ways in which the individualism, the stress on education and learning, the throwing-off of conventional practices, which marked the sixteenth century, are found in operation—of course in their special, perhaps limited mode—in the ideals and work of the society. But just as in the general society of the world the obverse of Renaissance individualism was Renaissance autocracy, so, in the Jesuit society, a new 'mode' of feeling rather, perhaps, than a new expression of principle hung about the traditional concept of religious obedience to superiors. It is quite true, and needs, I think, to be emphasised, that almost everything that is said in the constitutions of the Society of Jesus about the nature and extent of religious obedience can be paralleled in medieval texts, rules, or constitutions, from Cassian onwards to the Franciscans. *Quasi cadaver* and the simile of the stick or tool in another's hand do not strike any fundamentally new note. The main substance of the spiritual teaching on obedience, from the point of view of its spiritual value and profit, is the same. But there is, as it seems to me, with the Jesuits a difference of context and general climate of feeling, which reveals a certain development in regard to the idea of authority that parallels in the ecclesiastical sphere the new concepts of authority coming to be held in the sphere of the state, and which we see also in regard to the view of papal authority. Both the structure of the Society of Jesus and the evolution of its varied and manifold functions provide environments which have their counterparts in contemporary civil spheres. Compared with the elaborate constitutions of the friars, and especially the Dominicans; compared also with the constitutions of the Cistercians and the newer congregations of Black Benedictines, the elective, representative element in the society's constitution is weak. The general, it is true, is elected by the professed society of the four vows—those, that is, who, in addition to the usual three, have taken a fourth to go instantly to foreign missions on the Pope's order. But the election of the general is practically the sole specifically named occasion on which the general congregation of the whole professed society, with elected delegates from the different provinces, is bound to meet. For the rest, though the constitutions refer to certain things that cannot be done without the assent of a general congregation, thus to some extent limiting the powers of the general, and also lay down that extreme crises or difficulties may call for its summons, it is stated in many places that it is better for the general congregation to meet as little as possible. And it is specifically one of the arguments for the life tenure of the generalship, so long a stumbling-block to sixteenth-century opponents of the society, that it obviates frequent or regular general congregations. It is parliament as viewed by Henry VII rather than by Stubbs's Henry IV.

The monastic reforming movements of the fifteenth century had turned to the plan of temporary religious superiors as one of their planks, together with frequent general chapters of the houses or congregations, and regular visitations by outside superiors. It was one of the presuppositions, fully medieval in idea, underlying the conciliar movement, as applied in the sphere of monastic reform. The life general of the Jesuits was much more the counterpart of the idea of permanent unfettered personal leadership, so powerful in sixteenth-century politics. There are indications in the constitutions that St Ignatius was not wholly unconscious of sometimes taking a leaf or two out of civil society's book. Nevertheless, wide though the general's authority might be, it was limited, not so much by a constitutional or representative structure after the medieval pattern, but by certain specific limitations laid down in the written constitutions and, more significantly, by the general 'mind' of the constitutions and the society as a whole—a kind of special natural law, the law of the nature of the Society of Jesus. Therefore the normal devolution on to trusted subordinate superiors of many of the general's powers is recognised in the constitutions as inevitable and right, and the general is not exempt from having around him men specially entrusted to watch over his own conduct. Nothing, to my mind, could be less military than the spirit of the constitutions, so flexible are they, so accommodating, so mindful of the differences between individual human personalities, so full of appeals to charity and ordinary consideration. Yet, when all is said and done, it cannot, I think, be denied that, between them, the freedom from a set monastic routine as part of the essence of the life; the wide range, both functional and geographical, of possible employment within the society; the power to allocate novices to one or other of the different grades of permanent membership in the society; the absence of a highly articulated, constantly functioning elective or representative element; the declared object of a universal mission—all tended to create an environment in which the exercise of authority somehow took on new accretions, and generated a new spirit; which invested it with a new character, a new element of personal awe, in which something of the attitude of subject to renaissance monarch, private soldier to generalissimo, could be detected. Indeed, it went even deeper. The members of the society were in general required to uphold the special theological views of the society's leading theologians in any permitted difference of theological opinion: the views of Molina on Grace and free will being an outstanding example. Even more significant was the tradition that set in for the enforcing of the prayer-methods of the *Spiritual Exercises* at the expense of more contemplative ways of praying; the severe discouragement given to mystical contemplation, as a type of prayer unsuited to the active nature of the Jesuit institute, by Mercurian, Acquaviva, and later Jesuit authorities.[1] There was, then, a much more than military authority within the society. If I do not carry my point to excess, it is not so much the military as the political parallels which, to my mind, indicate the society as a true child of its age. Authority in the sixteenth-century state, in expanding the range of its interests and controls and claims, was inevitably beginning to shed the restraints of medieval constitutionalism, and to modify the medieval view of natural limitations, while at the same time giving increased scope to successful individuals under its ultimate control. Within the Society of Jesus, as at length within many of the modern congregations of priests modelled consciously or unconsciously upon it, new widths and manners of apostolate called for a more unencumbered functioning of the authority-obedience nexus of the 'religious state'; medieval stability in one house or abbey and medieval routines of communal liturgical prayer and medieval constitutional structures disappeared as a new versatility of activity and a necessary corresponding buttressing of private spiritual *Innerlichkeit* for the individual took their place.

I have perhaps spent too much time in examining the Society of Jesus as the classical example of this new, more flexible, type of religious community, and have not left much to deal with the other manifestations of this same theme. The 'congregation' idea, the institute of 'reformed' clerks, regular or secular, with or without the special characteristics that make the Society of Jesus unique, was plainly well calculated to promote the many active works that counter-reformation spirituality demanded. The universality of scope of the Jesuits was not, however, paralleled in any other institution—neither in the Theatines nor in the Oratorians, nor in any of the seventeenth-century congregations such as St Vincent's Priests of the Mission or the Eudists or the

[1] See above, p. 66 n.

de Montfort Fathers. But, speaking generally, the genius of the age did not permit the Jesuits to establish in any single sphere a complete monopoly, which they would not indeed have desired. The desire for better education for churchmen and laymen alike was a hallmark of the times, but St Ignatius and the Jesuit Constitutions do not seem in the first instance to have definitely contemplated general educational work for boys—what we should now call general secondary education—or to have felt a special educational mission, in our sense of the words, towards them. The reference in the Jesuit vows is to the instructing of boys in their religion, which admittedly was from the beginning a key point in the Jesuit programme, but the Jesuit speciality in ordinary secondary education (they never touched primary) was something which evolved naturally from the premises of their institute and from the turning towards them of public authorities which felt the need for schools and saw in the Jesuits men eminently fitted to provide them. The study of the early Jesuit schools, their origins, the sources of their tradition, their comparison with other contemporaneous educational systems, is far too large to be attempted here. But doubtless the prevalence and success of their schools was one of the influences that led to the development of what was, I think, quite new in the history of the Church, the founding of religious orders and congregations with the specific and sole object of school-teaching, regarded as a Christian work of charity through which the religious leading a regular life with the normal three vows sought both his own sanctification and the good of his neighbour. Neither Jesuits nor French Oratorians, for all the magnitude and success of their school work, were, to use a popular expression, 'teaching orders' in this exclusive sense. Nor, in the past, had been the Brothers of the Common Life. Some strivings in this direction had been made in Italy in the 1530s by St Angela Merici, though the original concept of her institute was not framed as the religious order it became.[1] There were a number of founders of small teaching congregations in the latter decades of the sixteenth

---

[1] Sister Monica, *Angela Merici and her teaching idea* (London, 1927); *Enciclopedia cattolica*, I, 122–3; Cistellini, above, p. 67 n.

century in France, and poor schools called the *Scuole della Dottrina Cristiana* were run in sixteenth-century Italy by the *compagnie* promoted by the priest Castellino da Castello. But the first exclusively 'teaching order' in the fullest sense would seem to be that of the Clerks Regular of the Pious Schools founded in Rome in 1597 by the Spaniard St Joseph Calasanctius, and confirmed as a definite regular congregation in 1621. Besides the three normal vows, the members took a fourth, to educate boys free of charge. The unhappy experience of the founder, who in 1646 witnessed the degradation of his institute, through the intrigues of one of its own members, to a lay institute, and did not live to see it restored to its pristine state in 1669, recalls the almost contemporary experiences of the great Englishwoman Mary Ward, whose struggles to take up again the original idea of St Angela and to found a teaching association of women bound by vows, 'religious', but not confined within an enclosure, and closely modelled on the Jesuits, met with such opposition that, though her foundation survived and today is a flourishing teaching order of nuns on modern lines, the founder's own official reputation at Rome was not rehabilitated until some fifty years ago.[1] The seventeenth century was not yet fully prepared for what was accomplished in the way of teaching orders, both male and female, in the nineteenth. In respect of women, enclosure was still regarded as essential. The legislation of the Council of Trent on the reform of convents takes strict enclosure for granted throughout. The wider, more active ambitions for nuns as teachers or well-doers, such as those of St Angela, Mary Ward, and St Jane Frances Chantal, either failed temporarily or became convents of enclosed nuns—Ursulines, Visitation nuns—on traditional lines. I can think of only one successful example, though it is an outstanding one: the Sisters of Charity of St Vincent de Paul.

Belonging properly to the last ripples of the Counter-Reformation in France, there is one further name and one further

---

[1] L. Hicks, 'Mary Ward's great enterprise', *The Month*, 1928–9; J. Grisar, *Die ersten Anklagen in Rom gegen das Institut Maria Wards* (Rome, 1959). See Postscript, p. 144.

foundation relevant to our subject which can hardly be omitted
—those of St John Baptist de la Salle and the teaching institute
of the Brothers of the Christian Schools. Exhaustively studied
in M. Rigault's large volumes,[1] and recently popularised in
England by the works of Dr Battersby, himself a brother of the
institute,[2] the Institute of St John Baptist is one of considerable
significance in both religious and educational history. This religious institute of men bound by vows but definitely not aspiring
to the priesthood, with its spiritual and social advantages, established in the modern world a vocation and a form of dedication
of remarkable idealism and practical difficulty, but one that has
spread widely and fruitfully in the modern world; it harks
back in some sense to the distinction between the monastic and
the priestly vocation seen in early monasticism, but now, among
the monks proper and the friars, hardly surviving at all, something
different from the distinction between choir monk and lay
brother. Such an institute as that of St John Baptist demanded
an intensive spirituality among its individual members and a high
degree of skill in organisation and management, and in both of
these the normal marks of the Counter-Reformation and the
influence of the Society of Jesus, much admired by de la Salle,
are visible. Educationally, St John Baptist paid unprecedented
attention to the proper technical training of the teacher, performing in this respect a role almost comparable to that of the
*Spiritual Exercises* in the spiritual sphere. Starting with elementary
schools, the brothers—and indeed all their spiritual descendants
in the many modern orders of brothers—widened in time the
scope of their activities, which now include also secondary
schools of grammar-school type, approved schools and schools
for defective children.

In the other great social activity into which the zeal of the
Counter-Reformation was poured—that of the care of the sick—
the creation of special institutes of religious persons was not so

[1] G. Rigault, *Histoire générale de l'Institut des Frères des Ecoles Chrétiennes* (9 vols.,
Paris, 1937–53).
[2] W. J. Battersby, *De la Salle: a pioneer of modern education* (London, 1949);
*De la Salle: saint and spiritual writer* (London, 1950). Also ed. by Battersby,
*De la Salle: letters and documents* (London, 1952).

novel as the creation of specific teaching orders, nor, probably, did the religious contribute so much to the profession in the way of technical progress. St Catherine of Genoa was hardly a fifteenth-century Florence Nightingale, but she did something to promote the technical side of nursing, as, certainly, did St Camillus of Lellis.[1] The two sixteenth-century foundations, of St Camillus in Rome—the Clerks Regular Ministers of the Sick—and of the Portuguese St John of God,[2] the latter based on the Augustinian rule, had had medieval prototypes in the Hospitallers and in various smaller orders dedicated to the sick, chiefly originating in the middle or late fourteenth century, perhaps as a result of the Black Death. Such were the Italian Jesuates, the Alexian Brothers, the German *Barmherzige Brüder*, and others. But, in the early sixteenth century, the French invasions of Italy had brought in their wake plagues the intensity and frequency of which it is difficult to appreciate, and which at least one modern authority regards as having reduced the population of the Italian cities by twenty-five or thirty per cent. In addition there had been introduced the dreaded syphilis, or *morbo gallico*, considered incurable and thought to have originated in America. A new stimulus, comparable to that of the Black Death, was given to hospital work. All the Italian oratories, including the Roman Oratory of Divine Love, whether or not deriving from the inspiration of St Catherine of Genoa, founded or helped in hospitals, especially for the *incurabili* whom normal hospitals refused to take, leaving these unfortunates to beg or die, and often both, in the streets. The early Jesuit attention to hospitals and hospital work, which was an essential feature of the early noviciate, was perhaps characterised more by a spiritual than by a purely medical approach, but the comfort, if not the healing, of the sick, as a good work, was heavily emphasised by all the Catholic spiritual leaders of the time. Sixteenth-century hospitals were not modern nursing homes. The hospitals of the day with all their unpleasantnesses and sordidness and crudeness were an environment into which the Counter-Reformation sought

---

[1] *Enciclopedia cattolica*, III, 438–9.
[2] *Ibid.* VI, 554–5.

to introduce the teachings and comforts of religion, and in which the exercise of the virtues of devotion, charity, tolerance and both mental and physical self-control might pre-eminently be cultivated.

There is not time to pursue further this general theme of the development during the Counter-Reformation of education and nursing, as material for men and women seeking to follow at the same time the evangelical counsels of perfection under the normal three monastic vows. The nineteenth century saw an enormous proliferation of such communities, so much so that they seem to be one of the outstanding hallmarks of the modern, post-Revolution Catholic Church. We may, however, legitimately see their true origins in the period of the Counter-Reformation, when the trend from contemplation to apostolate was so marked.

# 5

# INSTITUTIONAL
# REFORM[1]

In my last lecture, when we were considering the new forms of
the communal religious life to which the Counter-Reformation
gave rise, we were in fact on territory where the two special
aspects of our general subject which I stressed in my opening
lecture—that of spirituality and that of institutional development
—may be said to meet, and the last lecture was indeed one of
transition from spiritual to institutional topics in this course.
Having previously dealt with Jesuit spirituality, I tried to present
a suggestion of the structure and organisation of the Society of
Jesus as reflecting, in a religious and ecclesiastical mode, the
newer climate of political thinking and acting which was at that
same time prevalent in the general political life of the western
European states. Today I want to try to carry that idea still
further, and to indicate how we may recognise it as applicable and
valid in the reorganisation and administration of the counter-
reformation Church as a whole. It is possible, I believe, to see
in the reorganisation of the government of the ecclesiastical body
remaining under Rome, with conscious uninterrupted continuity
from the medieval Church in the west, a process reflecting the
reorganisation of contemporary states, and to envisage the twin
processes as in some sort, and *mutatis mutandis*, due to the
same kind of causes, necessities and conditions.

The parallels in method between civil and ecclesiastical
government in the middle ages are too obvious to be stressed.
Despite the mystic interpenetration of Church and state in the

---

[1] For the general subject discussed in this and the following lecture, see, apart
from Pastor, H. E. Feine, *Kirchliche Rechtsgeschichte*, Bd. 1: *Die katholische Kirche*
(2nd ed. Weimar, 1954), esp. pp. 463-96, and W. M. Plöchl, *Geschichte des Kirchenrechts*, III, part 1 (Vienna/Munich, 1959)—longer, very comprehensive and with
larger bibliographies, but rather a work of reference than a history. The relevant
volume in G. le Bras (ed.), *Histoire du droit et des institutions de l'Eglise en
Occident* (Paris, 1955-) has not yet appeared.

notion of the unity and oneness of Christendom, the Church was nevertheless a distinct society with her own functions of an administrative, a juridical, a financial, even a purely political kind; and for all these purposes she created organs and tribunals and sets of officials which paralleled those of the civil order— and in a sense inevitably so, for neither can be represented as having specifically copied the other. The evolution at Rome of the papal court—at once domestic, ceremonial and governmental —with all its development of secretariats, departments and tribunals for carrying on the central business of Church administration, and in a smaller way the evolution of episcopal courts, paralleled the similar evolution of the royal courts and the baronial courts of the European monarchies. The medieval Church possessed many of the attributes of the state, in some respects in a more advanced and effective form than the 'states' themselves and operative certainly over a wider—indeed so far as theory went it was a universal—geographical area. The subject-matter of the Roman courts and departments consisted, in theory, of religious affairs and the affairs of clerics everywhere; many affairs with spiritual implication or significance concerning laymen; and, as administration and finance became more centralised, especially in the fourteenth and fifteenth centuries, the holding and interchanging of Church offices—ecclesiastical benefices of all sorts—with all the economic concomitants of this: a vast range of assorted business, ranging from purely spiritual and religious matters downwards to affairs in which the material and the economic side loomed large. Through the organs of the papal curia the papacy as an institution administered, appointed, judged and taxed; as, for example, the English kingship did through the many organs of *its* curia.

In comparing Church and state in this way in the middle ages, and while realising that under medieval conditions all administration, by whomsoever done, must almost inevitably have been done in the same sort of way, by institutions evolving from the domestic to the political, we must nevertheless take into account some necessary distinctions. Within the Church considered as a visible society of a political nature there existed what civil society lacked: the recognition of a true legal sovereign. The ecclesiastical Canon Law recognised in the Pope a sovereign person, supreme source and interpreter of the Canon Law in his own right, by virtue of his office of successor to St Peter, and not by virtue of any form of popular delegation. Because this was so, the Church was spared, broadly speaking, the internal constitutional struggles and the institutional conflicts that beset civil society, not merely in the middle ages, but also later. Again, because this was so, the papacy was able to preserve its own original control over the whole complicated bureaucracy that was spun out of its court in the middle ages and, later, over the new bureaucracy of congregations of cardinals which it created in the sixteenth century. It was limited in the extent of its control of all these bodies only by the inherent independent strengths which a developed bureaucracy with vested interests and set procedures naturally creates for itself even against its political masters, and which was excessively strong in the papal curia from 1450 to 1550. It was not limited in its control over its own organs by any representative body claiming to represent some power theoretically superior to itself or able in fact to muster a physical force more powerful than that at its own disposal. The representative principle, indeed, existed within the Church, for example in provincial and diocesan organisation, and in the constitutions of the religious orders; and it has been maintained by some in the past that ecclesiastical representation partly inspired civil representation. But organised representation in the ecclesiastical sphere had only a limited range and limited functions; and in the overall papal administration of the middle ages it had no place at all. The general council of all the bishops was called by the papacy at its own will and for its own purposes. It did not evolve into anything like a secular parliament, and it possessed no financial or political lever.

We must not, of course, represent things too simply. The idea that all authority of whatsoever kind must in the last analysis have a popular origin was embedded deep in the subconsciousness of the middle ages, and was also of course found in the theory of the Roman Civil Law. The belief that in the last resort the ultimate authority in the Church lay in the general body of Christendom as a whole, and might be made articulate through a general council, however defined, was not, it would seem, invented during the great schism—nor, perhaps, deliberately copied from secular models. It seems to have had definite earlier existence, no doubt of a rather speculative, academic kind, and to have acted perhaps as a kind of running subconscious query appended to the full-blooded canonist theory of papal sovereignty, long before the events of the schism and the irritation of the fourteenth and fifteenth centuries with the centralisation of Rome —ever increasing, and abusively so—gave occasion for the elaboration and popularisation of 'conciliar' theories regarding the nature and 'Constitution' of the Church. I speak here much under correction, as a clumsy trespasser treading gingerly in the enclosed garden of the medievalists. But I would like to refer to a recent and profoundly interesting article by B. Tierney, entitled 'A Conciliar Theory of the Thirteenth Century'.[1] This shows that in the works of—*mirabile dictu!*—one of the greatest thirteenth-century canonists, Hostiensis himself, there is to be found put forward a view of the Church not as a single society under a sovereign head but as a hierarchy of corporations in which ultimate authority rests with the whole body of the faithful; followed up by a theory of Church government and organisation in terms very similar to those applied several decades later to the state by Marsiglio of Padua: in fact, if I have it right, Marsiglio's doctrine of the sanction of authority and the structure of power in the secular state anticipated for the Church by a canon lawyer, and not only anticipated but worked out much more fully and without Marsiglio's obscurities! In watching the further flowering of supreme papal action during the Counter-Reformation we must not forget the subtleties and complexities of the medieval past.

For, in fact, what the Counter-Reformation brought to the Church was a new flowering of papal supremacy, with the older academic queries and complexity of views fading away. Not so

[1] *Catholic Historical Review*, xxxvi (1951), 415-40; and now *Foundations of the conciliar theory* (Cambridge, 1955).

much by virtue of any new definition as by the vigorous taking
of action when action was necessary, executive power brushed
aside speculative uncertainties about its competence: such
action as was the reply of all vigorous sixteenth-century executives
to the opportunities and the crises of the epoch—the action of
a Henry VIII, an Elizabeth, an Henri Quatre. For the parallels
between the developing patterns of secular and ecclesiastical
government do not end with the middle ages. They continue
into the post-medieval era, though there they have perhaps been
less frequently marked, or at least less adequately analysed.
Indeed, I would go further and say that at any given historical
moment the methods and spirit of all administration tend to be
similar, whether it is Church or state that is being administered;
and that if we care to consider the matter objectively we may
well find that this is as true today as ever. I am not here concerned,
however, with the present (which tomorrow, however, will be
history) but with the past. The sixteenth-century counterpart,
in Catholicism, of what used to be called the new monarchy
is the counter-reformation papacy, not only in general spirit
but also in precise method: the taking into papal hands of all
the new tasks that the Counter-Reformation in all its aspects
required; enforcement of the Tridentine decrees; establishment
of new relations with secular powers; extension of mission work
in heathen lands; reorganisation of pastoral and controversial
equipment in Europe, and the counter-attacks on Protestantism.
All this involved, not only the restoration of the failing or misused
forces of older-created institutions, but also the articulation of
new organs of government, more appropriate to the new tasks, the
employment of new servants and so forth, all combined with the
skilful holding in check of all the forces of internal opposition
to the papal fullness of power. If the Council of Trent could not
bring itself officially to echo the definition of Florence and hail
the Pope in a decree as *Rector Universalis Ecclesiae*, the counter-
reformation papacy had no hesitation in acting as if it had done
so. Like the secular realms, the counter-reformation Church
needed a stronger executive power, with free initiative and un-
hampered discretion, capable of controlling all the activities of

the society subject to it, stimulating here, discouraging there, dealing with emergencies and unprecedented situations. And like the secular monarchies the papacy also required a new financial basis. Between 1520 and about 1600 it gradually lost the bulk of its precious revenue derived from taxation of all the Churches of western Christendom, and from the profits of the curial departments made through the disposal of benefices and the granting of dispensations and favours. Instead, it recouped itself by developing, indeed by overstraining, the taxable resources of the papal states, now more and more reduced to a manageable political unit on more modern lines, by the development of a remarkably advanced system of public credit in the loans known as *monti*,[1] and also—as every other government did—by reliance on loans from bankers. Italian bankers, principally Florentine and Genoese, continued to manage basic papal finance; the Fuggers had only dealt with German business. The efforts of the renaissance Popes to enlarge and consolidate the states of the Church—whatever the moral situation might be—were in the practical sphere amply justified in the eyes of their counter-reformation successors. Without Julius II could there have been a Sixtus V? At the end of the sixteenth century, when, according to Braudel's interesting thesis, empires declined and the hour of the small state struck,[2] the papal state was among the latter.

Before looking more closely at the positive side of the development of the papal ecclesiastical government, it might help to glance at certain attendant but only slightly hampering difficulties. Professor Jedin, in his *History of the Council of Trent*, has summarised the history of conciliar thought and conciliar attempts from the Council of Basle to the Lateran Council of 1512–16.[3] The failure of the conciliar movement to limit the papal sovereignty by grafting the general council on to the

---

[1] J. Delumeau, *Vie économique et sociale de Rome pendant la deuxième moitié du xvi<sup>e</sup> siècle* (2 vols., Rome, 1957–9), esp. II, 751–843; see Postscript, pp. 142–4.

[2] Braudel, *La Méditerranée et le monde méditerranéen à l'époque de Philippe II*, pp. 546 f.

[3] Jedin, *History of the Council of Trent*, I, 1–138.

constitutional life of the Church as a regularly occurring piece of machinery did not leave the papacy in the later fifteenth century with any feelings of absolute and secure triumph. Conciliarism had, indeed, inevitably killed itself by its ineptitudes and inconsistencies, but it was still an idea to be played with and a threat capable on occasion of causing alarm in Rome. The occasions threatened to recur more alarmingly when the growing cry for the reform of the Church in head and members, and still more the profound crisis brought about by the development of Protestantism, created situations in which a general council seemed in the highest degree necessary. But Protestantism, by revolutionising the concept of the Church, also revolutionised the concept of a general council as understood by the papacy. Even a general council within the medieval convention, however, seemed to carry some danger for the papacy. This danger in actual fact came not so much from the possible revival of old academic constitutional claims as from the alliance between conciliarist doctrine and the practical claims of the secular powers. The schismatic Council of Pisa, in some ways a last display of medieval fireworks by turbulent cardinals, was nevertheless significant as an example of such an alliance between secular political claims and ecclesiastical theories. A graver danger than that of pure conciliarism threatened the papacy from the claim of the secular power to direct ecclesiastical policy, and to do this through its influence over its own bishops, so largely state nominees, at a general council. To some extent, of course, this had always been so. The whole history of the Council of Trent illustrates how much it was so in the sixteenth century. The manner in which first Charles V and then, after 1559, the French crown tried to use the Council of Trent to force upon the papacy the acceptance of their own special formulae for settling the religious and politico-religious troubles of Germany and France respectively carried with it ultimately a danger of the Church becoming divided up into a mosaic of state-controlled national or regional Churches, each evolving its own brand of liturgy and worship, and no doubt, ultimately, doctrine too, according to the political needs of the moment or the need to appease reformation movements. I am inclined myself to think that here we see the gravest of all the internal threats to the unity of Roman Catholicism that existed at that moment, and one that was only overcome by the revival of independence and strength in the episcopate in alliance with the reinvigoration and expansion of the Roman supremacy. At Trent the papacy, with remarkable diplomatic skill, and inspired by an unshakable conviction of the righteousness of its cause, not only thwarted the drift towards a variety of national settlements under the pressure of political motives but even laid the foundations of an even more complete liturgical and disciplinary, as well as dogmatic, uniformity in the western Churches under its rule. It is necessary to see the clash of points of view as objectively as we can. If this political issue of control was vital for the Church, the religious issue was vital for the state, and the failure of force to reimpose uniformity of belief left the state in an awkward position *vis-à-vis* a Church which continued to demand the impossible.

I am not here primarily concerned with this nevertheless fundamental counter-reformation issue of Church and state, the echoes of which have rumbled throughout the succeeding centuries. I pass now to the first main positive achievement of papacy and Trent in the sphere of Church administration, the restoration of the efficiency of the episcopate.

The reforms of the Council of Trent assumed without question the maintenance of the existing Church structure, constitutional, economic, jurisdictional: the organisation of ecclesiastical provinces, dioceses, chapters, collegiate and parish churches; the hierarchy of ecclesiastical persons—cardinals, primates, archbishops, canons, prebendaries, rectors, vicars, curates and so forth; the existing classification of benefices—with cure of souls, without cure of souls, simple, complex—with all the different claims on their revenues; the religious orders with their own varying constitutional structures and their different degrees of exemption from episcopal control. All these formed a complicated web of persons and institutions with rights and duties, interests and obligations, according to the provisions of Canon Law and ecclesiastical tradition. From an institutional and juridical point of view, the machine was clogged in its workings by its own medieval elaborateness; it was liable to be constantly thrown out of gear by the *deus ex machina* of supreme Roman authority, capable of intervening at almost every point, and not always for the best, through the various persons, officials and tribunals of the Roman court. Most deadly of all, the attractions of the Church as a career not only for the highly intelligent, the erudite or the avaricious but also, *faute des autres*, for the average normal man anxious to secure a livelihood acted like a vampire sucking at the spiritual life-blood that should have pulsated through the Church's veins and ensured the employment of all the complex machinery for the prime and basic purpose for which it all existed. In the social and economic conditions of the time, which were only slowly being modified in the sixteenth century, it was well-nigh impossible to obviate these dangers. Short of a complete economic as well as ecclesiastical revolution, short of a modern system of salaries paid by a central body— secular or ecclesiastical, Church or state—the benefice system of ecclesiastical property and revenues as the basis of clerical maintenance had for Catholicism no alternative. A radically Franciscan solution for the whole Church was visionary and impractical; a state ownership of all ecclesiastical property had deadly implications.

The reformers at the Council of Trent did not begin to question the need for the maintenance of the whole fabric of the traditional ecclesiastical world. They did not even consider how it might perhaps be simplified. They were not revolutionaries. There was too much revolution already about in Europe. They sought, however, to guard against practical abuses and, with remarkable faith, to reinstill into the whole machine the true pastoral apostolic spirit. All their efforts centred round the restoration of the episcopate, morally and administratively; and the strengthening of the episcopate in every respect, as the nodal point of every aspect of reform, may be regarded as a corner-stone of the counter-reformation Church. The reassertion of the primacy of the pastoral over against the only too generally held view of bishoprics as titular honours, bringing revenue, to be given as rewards and favours for personal or political purposes, called for a new attitude—a new method, where possible—in the selection of bishops. It called for the residence of bishops in their dioceses, rather than at the courts of princes or Popes. It demanded that their episcopal attention should be given wholeheartedly to their duties towards their flock, rather than to diplomacy, secular administration, art, letters, leisure or even learning. If they were to be successful at their task they must not find themselves constantly confronted by persons or corporate bodies exempt from their jurisdiction and able to continue in obstructive or reprehensible ways, often through recourse to the curia at Rome. All these things the council tried to effect, or at least to encourage where it could do no more. Careful regulations for the selection of bishops were laid down, but it was recognised, somewhat sadly, that where the secular authorities had, by concordat or custom, the privilege of nominating to the Pope for appointment —and that was in large parts of Europe—all the council could do was gravely to exhort them to nominate suitable men. Yet, if bishoprics had not been so valuable financially and socially, it would not have come about that in so many countries in Europe the right of nomination had passed into the state's hands. The duty of residence, besides involving theoretical issues to which I shall recur in a minute, also raised the question of pluralities and accumulation. It was not uncommon for several bishoprics, in some cases even up to double figures, and possibly strewn over several countries, to be held by a single man, or for one man to have rights of pension, or of regress, in as many. This the council utterly forbade—as Popes had done before—and although the habit of pluralism was long in dying out, especially in Germany, owing to the still-remaining possibilities of dispensation, by the end of the sixteenth century the corner had been turned. The changing climate of opinion, as the tide of reform rose steadily and perceptibly, helped the council's decrees to become effective. Cardinals had been particular offenders; but as more and more cardinals came to be drawn from the circles under reform influences, compliance with reform's demands increased.

The Jesuits have been called the maids-of-all-work of the Counter-Reformation. They at least, for the most part, chose their own works. The bishops had everything thrust upon them.[1] It was in the nature of their office. By the decrees of the Council of Trent they must not leave their dioceses for more than a short time without permission; they must preach regularly; conduct annual visitations; hold annual synods; attend provincial synods every three years; superintend hospitals and charitable organisations; found seminaries; ordain only persons suitably educated, trained and examined; correct moral faults and administrative abuses; punish where appropriate; root out concubinage in the clergy; mark out parishes; see to the appropriate staffing of parishes; give licences for preaching, even to members of religious orders; keep a fatherly eye on convents; deal with the misdemeanours of regulars living outside their convents; redistribute the income of offices and benefices where necessary; introduce all the new reforms and changes in the Canon Law (a modern canonist has counted two hundred and fifty); give an example in dress, behaviour, charity, modesty—and no doubt, by implication, good temper. It was no sinecure episcopal office that the fathers at Trent envisaged. But it was not an impossible one. Examples had already been given and were soon to multiply. Giberti of Verona had been outstanding, and his example was powerful and persuasive. Others outstanding were Bartholomew de Martyribus, archbishop of Braga in Portugal; Fisher of Rochester in England; Carlo Borromeo in Milan; Alessandro Santi, a Barnabite, bishop of Aleria in Corsica; and a number of other Italians, many influenced by the Theatine fathers, whose congregation was a fertile nursery of Italian counter-reformation bishops. In Spain there was Thomas of Villanueva, in Savoy at the end of the century François de Sales. Trent was no doubt right to aim at a high episcopal ideal.

For a long time the controversy between the bishops and the orders had raged. It had come to a head in the Lateran Council

---

[1] H. Jedin, *Il tipo ideale di vescovo secondo la riforma cattolica* (Brescia, 1950): translation of *Das Bischofsideal der katholischen Reformation*; French version by P. Broutin, *L'évêque dans la tradition pastorale du xvi<sup>e</sup> siècle* (Bruges, 1953).

under Julius II and Leo X, and the bishops had not come out of it very well, or very successfully. How, said the bishops, can we restore order and decency in our dioceses if the regulars with their exemptions from episcopal control, granted at Rome, monopolise so much of the spiritual work—preaching, confessions, and so forth—without check or licence or hindrance? Why, retorted the regulars, should it be necessary for us to undertake so much pastoral work, except that the bishops neglect their dioceses and do not provide for it themselves? And indeed there were those realists at Trent, and at Rome, who asked whether, while secular-minded bishops were appointed, it was 'not better for them to keep clear of their dioceses and leave the work to paid vicars and assistants, as was so commonly done. But the vital principle of reuniting in one person the duties and the profits of all ecclesiastical benefices was upheld at Trent and, indeed, was a fundamental point to be insisted upon in regard to all Church benefices, from papacy to parish. The troubled question of the exemption of regulars, collegiate churches, chapters and other institutions was solved by putting them under the bishop's power, as might be necessary and appropriate for reasons of general decency and practical efficiency, but with the bishop, however, often acting as papal delegate—for there is no exemption from the papacy! I have counted nearly thirty instances in the Tridentine reform decrees in which the bishop is empowered to act as papal delegate. This was not a subtle device to increase papal power and prestige at the expense of episcopal. It was, in general, a way of reconciling the principle of exemption with the necessity of modifying it substantially in practice. It was also laid down that all dispensations obtained at Rome should be obtained and received through the bishop. This was aimed at preventing the constant side-stepping of episcopal reforms which would otherwise doubtless have continued in plenty.

Thus the duties, importance and prestige of the bishop's office in the whole work of the Church and in the development of the Counter-Reformation were *de facto* all much enlarged. But the increase in practice of episcopal powers and prestige was accompanied by a persisting ambiguity in respect of the theory of the episcopate.[1] The divine right of the episcopate was uncontested in the sense that the territorial office itself, as well as the apostolic succession of the sacramental episcopal orders as the fullness of the priesthood, were both held to be divinely ordained, but the exact relation of the papacy in regard to the exercise of the episcopal office by each particular bishop was disputed. The issue arose at the Council of Trent over the question of enforcing residence. Was it divine law which commanded a bishop to reside in his see? Or only Canon Law? If the former, then no dispensation was possible, even by the Pope. The debate was carried a stage further when the chapters on the doctrine of the sacrament of holy orders were being discussed. Was the episcopal jurisdiction—as distinct from the sacramental powers of holy orders—of each bishop in his diocese given him by immediate divine right when appointed or consecrated? Or did his jurisdiction come mediately through the Pope? That the debates over these matters nearly wrecked the council in 1562 and 1563 is well known—the episcopal party drawing its strength not only from the French, Spanish and other non-Italian prelates but from a considerable number of Italians too. The opposition of the French prevented the insertion into the decree of the phrase accepted even by the orientals at the Council of Florence referring to the Pope as *Rector Universalis Ecclesiae*. There was no sufficient basis of agreement for a definition. In the end residence was enjoined, but *de quo jure* was left unspecified. The chapters of doctrine concerning the episcopate were content to state as Catholic doctrine that 'bishops are placed by the Holy Ghost to rule the Church of God' and that they 'have succeeded to the place of the Apostles'. But though saved from being declared no more than mere delegates of the Pope, there were more and more instances in which the bishops had to act, and behave, as such.

The bishops constituted an organ in the Church to which we can find no real equivalent in the world of secular politics. Yet, for all the acknowledged divine sanction of their origin and status (whatever precisely the latter might be!), their practical

[1] On which see now the work of Alberigo discussed below, Postscript, pp. 135 f.

position *vis-à-vis* the expanding and deepening papal sovereignty, through the struggle of Gallicanism, Josephism, Febronianism, Cisalpinism and so on, right up to the Vatican Council, may perhaps not unsignificantly be compared to the gradual enfeeblement throughout modern times of the natural-right claims of local communities or interests against central sovereign power. The Counter-Reformation, partly by design, partly through the play of natural forces, both restored the Catholic episcopate to new efficiency and weakened its institutional independence; and it was the same forces that effected both results.

If the exact status of bishops in the Church *vis-à-vis* the papal *plenitudo potestatis* still remained in theory somewhat undetermined, no such ambiguity hung about the position of the curial offices in Rome.[1] They were the direct organs of papal power; and despite the outcry against them and the charge freely brought against them of being responsible for a great part of the ills and misfortunes of the Church as a whole, the counter-reformation papacy, while anxious in due course to effect suitable reforms in their working, succeeded in protecting them from either reform or destruction at the hands of any other power, whether councils or secular potentates. The organs of the curia were criticised on more than one score. In the first place they stood for an extreme centralisation of all sorts of ecclesiastical business, especially concerning appointments to benefices, which in an age of developing nationalism was felt to be increasingly undesirable and unnatural by non-Italians. Secondly, their methods were at many places open to the charges not only of slowness and chicanery but of direct corruption, and not only were they unpopular for their part in the imposition and administration of the many taxes, charges, fees and payments of all kinds which the papacy drew from all parts of the Church, but also, in the eyes of reformers, because their whole spirit and method deepened the general 'secularisation' of the concept of the ecclesiastical benefice. By reason of the many devious ways in which benefices

[1] W. von Hofmann, *Forschungen zur Geschichte der kurialen Behörden vom Schisma bis zur Reformation* (2 vols., Rome, 1914); cf., on curial opposition to reform, H. Jedin, *Tommaso Campeggio (1483-1564): tridentinische Reform und kuriale Tradition* (Münster, 1958), pp. 20-3, 73-6.

could be accumulated in defiance of the law, exchanged, handed on, taken back, earmarked, made subject to pensions—in fact the whole complex of reservations, regressions, expectations, and so forth—the whole machine assumed something of the air of a kind of expensive but necessary and unavoidable exchange agency where money could be placed with a view to a return in interest, and the investments almost bought and sold, with little attention to the pastoral duties which were attached to so many (but not all) of the ecclesiastical offices and dignities concerned. The economic livelihood of a whole new class of men all over Europe was concerned in this business, while a large and increasing class in Rome lived on its administration. The heavy financial commitments of the papacy called for the continuance of the system. Many and acute were the views expressed by people of different degrees of attachment to the idea of reform, as to whether and, if so, exactly where the sin or simony could be pinned down as occurring in all these transactions; and subtle distinctions, involving the mental separation of the ecclesiastical office from the endowment going with it, were put forward as the basis of explanations calculated to rebuff the charge. And bound up with this traffic and the problems raised by critics as to its simoniacal character was another main accusation levelled at the papal curia as a whole: its easy and inexhaustible capacity for providing dispensations from almost any and every canonical obligation, to the ruin of Church order and to the promotion of scandal.

All this was much intensified in the period of the High Renaissance. Starting roughly with the pontificate of Sixtus IV, further developments occurred which ushered in the period of maximum odium for the papal curia and which still further accelerated the outward flow of dispensations and favours and the inward flow of money, pushing to their culminating point the secularisation and venality of the whole machine. These developments comprised first the appearance of yet new tribunals and officers who dispensed papal favours and dispensations or all sorts, cutting across the not too well differentiated spheres of action of older departments; and secondly the growth of the number of employees in the curia as the sale of offices became, for the papacy, a recognised source of revenue such as it was later to become for the kings of France and Spain and the sultan of Turkey.

There were first the two tribunals known as the *signaturae*—equity tribunals, as it were, through which the Pope was approached direct and in which he signed, or originally signed, the petitions brought to him. Innocent VIII separated the *referendarii* who helped the Pope when it was a matter of pure favour from those whose business was to advise him when a point of law was involved. Hence the distinction between the *signatura gratiae* and the *signatura justitiae*, the latter becoming a properly constituted tribunal. Secondly, there occurred between Martin V and Julius III a considerable development in the functions of the papal *datarius*, or 'datary', and his assistants, who formed yet another channel through which special papal gifts of benefices, dispensations, honours, dignities, privileges, or other favours could be obtained. The 'datary' and his helpers were not formally constituted into a department, the *dataria*, until 1588. The *datarius* came to have financial functions too, in assessing and exacting the heavy and hated payments called *compositiones*. Many points in the office's history remain obscure despite the study of its origins by Léonce Célier,[1] no doubt because it was for long a question of the functions of an individual officer closely in touch with the Pope and not of an office proper. It had no archives until 1672. But it was these renaissance inventions for extra-legal papal favour-bestowing, the *signaturae* and datary, which came to be the most roundly criticised elements in the whole curia in the early and middle sixteenth century, on account of the way in which all kinds of dispensations were given which thwarted so many aspects of reform, and, in the case of the datary, also for its financial extortion. But up to the middle of the sixteenth century the profits of the datary were held essential for the papal budget. Datary and *signaturae*, however, were not alone in their abuse of dispensations, for even the penitentiary was attacked by the reformers at Rome for the manner in which

[1] *Les dataires du xvᵉ siècle et les origines de la Daterie Apostolique* (Paris, 1910).

its various licences stood in the way of the reform of the religious orders.

But there was yet another aspect of the predominance of finance at Rome which reached its peak between 1470 and 1529. As the acquisition and accumulation of benefices was the livelihood of many all over Europe, so the acquisition of posts in the curia became that of a class in Rome. The whole story of the multiplication of posts and offices in the curia and their being practically put up for sale has been examined by W. von Hofmann in his massive and erudite researches into the history of the curial officials from the schism to the Reformation.[1] The technique and development of all this, the organisation of the officials in colleges with their rights and privileges, reveals the pursuit by the renaissance papacy of a policy of creation and sale of offices which later was to obtain in France and Spain and elsewhere: a policy by which the central power obtained relief to its budget, and a growing official class acquired life-maintenance or 'life-annuities' which a policy of reform would undermine. As all this developed from about Sixtus IV onwards, the venality penetrating upwards into even the highest offices, the former international character of the curia gradually diminished; the element in it of laymen or married clerks in minor orders decreased, and an almost wholly Italian clerical body found its livelihood in the maintenance of the full working of the papal court.

The papal curia and its departments have been much studied up to the sack of Rome. But no one, so far as I know, has yet tried to give an overall account of their history from that time onwards until, by about the turn of the sixteenth century, or the early years of the seventeenth, they seem to have reached again a point of stability when it becomes possible for treatises describing in some detail their manner of working to be written. By that time certain of them had been considerably reformed and cut down, though none had been radically altered; and, what is more, the financial importance to the papacy of the datary, and in general of money drawn from Churches outside Italy, had diminished. Pope and cardinals between them, helped by some

[1] See p. 102 n.; also discussed by Delumeau (see p. 94 n.).

decrees of the Council of Trent, effected some reform, but there was no institutional revolution. The real attempts at reform begin, as with so much else, under Paul III. Whereas the papal records under Clement VII reveal little in the way of reform endeavours, with Paul III there begins a series of draft reforms, draft bulls, appointments of commissions, and opinions of consultors, which goes on throughout the pontificates of Julius III and Paul IV. The great question of the exact definition of simony was much discussed but never officially answered. A compromise was eventually worked out between the reformers of the *Consilium de Emendanda Ecclesia* of 1537 on the one hand, who wished for very radical structural change and did not fear to accept the position that much was being tolerated that was simoniacal, and on the other the conservatives, who had a way of defending the *status quo* by involving the traditional fear of the thin end of the wedge and the shame of a public admission of papal simony. Gradually the number of unnecessary officials was reduced. The pressure, against heavy and skilful opposition from the vested interests concerned,[1] of Paul III, Julius III and Paul IV had some effects. Mandosi's treatise on the *signatura gratiae* in 1558 seems to show that the worst dispensations earlier given in this tribunal had come to an end. Though the decrees of the first two meetings at Trent were too mild, and certainly proved ineffectual, in 1563 many of the devices concerning the revenues of benefices which had encouraged the extremes of fiscality were abolished. Professor Jedin believes that as early as 1564 the financial motive in the much criticised datary had been heavily reduced, at any rate in comparison with the period 1480–1530.[2] Pius V entirely suppressed the penitentiary and re-established it on reformed lines. Thus, when we get to the reign of Gregory XIII and approach that of Sixtus V, it is possible to suppose that the trio of penitentiary, *signaturae* and datary were no longer what they had been.

We are getting now, however, into a period when the whole moral atmosphere at Rome is changing, when the spirit of

---

[1] A more sympathetic view is taken by Jedin, in *Tommaso Campeggio* (see p. 102 n.).
[2] I think this suggestion may have been privately communicated.

ecclesiastical decency and order has revived with a new generation, when the spiritual work of the Theatines and Jesuits in Rome, and also of St Philip Neri, has had its results, even among the curial class—from minor officials up to cardinals. But, in addition to this, the emphasis in church government is changing, with the development of new counter-reformation interests and activities in the papacy; and both the political and the economic conditions are fast altering. The normal routine offices descending from the medieval curia settle down to their normal necessary business, somewhat purged in spirit, reduced in numbers, and deprived of many former dangerous occasions of venality. The purely renaissance blossomings of papal bounty and reform-thwarting dispensations have faded; and though the economic attractions of bishoprics and abbeys remain, and pluralism and accumulation do not die out completely, they become less and less a matter of course. The notion of high office in the Church as something intrinsically valuable from an economic point of view was indeed difficult to drop, so long as the sources of ecclesiastical wealth remained unconfiscated by the state and protected from severe depreciation. But with Gregory XIII, Sixtus V and their successors, the papacy is concerned in a new way with larger policies. It is with these, and with the new organs evolved to deal with them, that I shall now be concerned.

# 6

## THE NEW ORGANS OF CHURCH GOVERNMENT

In considering the reorganisation of government that took place in the counter-reformation Church, I have dealt mainly with the moral and administrative revival of the episcopate, or at least the principle on which this was attempted, and with the elimination of the worst abuses and unnecessary elaborations of the various departments in the Roman curia. Bishops and curia, however, were long-established, accepted institutions, and in the course of my preliminary, more general remarks I said, more than once, that the development of the papal sovereignty by administrative and executive action led to the creation of new organs, in the evolution of which a certain parallel between papal and monarchical, in the patterns of their administration, may again be seen. The first instance of this is in the history of the cardinals, who from their first appearance had formed, in a looser and wider sense, a part of the papal 'court'. But at the end of the fifteenth century the cardinals may be said to have stood to the Pope very much as a turbulent and obstructive baronage to a medieval king. They were, in a sense, his natural advisers, part of his court, but they were neither suitably appointed nor properly organised for appropriate advice-giving. They were frequently divided into opposing factions which obstructed the discussion of business in the consistory; while some sincere churchmen and reformers were found among them, they represented more often than not the interests of foreign states or great Italian families, and some resided permanently outside Rome. As a body they stood *par excellence* for the system of accumulation and exploitation of bishoprics and other ecclesiastical benefices, especially non-Italian benefices, for financial profit. As renaissance patrons of art they could vie with the Pope himself. As politicians they were sometimes known even to conspire against his life. But they had the supreme privilege of electing him from among their own numbers, though the cardinal so elected was universally accustomed, despite the capitulations of the conclave, to drop instantaneously any previous views he might have had concerning the rights of the cardinals to a real co-partnership in the possession of papal power. Up to the great creation of Leo X in 1517 their numbers were small: the first conclave to have more than twenty participants was that of Innocent VIII in 1484; and as the fifteenth century drew to its close the college became, like the papal curia in general, more and more Italian, less and less international in composition.

It was, however, always a weakness of the cardinal body that no one could say for certain exactly what was its true constitutional position in either the Roman Church in the local sense, or the Catholic Church as a whole. The various plans put forward for the 'reform' of the cardinals throughout the fifteenth and first half of the sixteenth centuries show this quite clearly. But the pattern of growing, engulfing sovereignty dominating and subduing lesser authorities by administrative action applies here too. By the end of the sixteenth century the papacy, without any theoretical clarification of the cardinals' position, had made good its long-maintained claim that they were papal creations, and therefore papal servants, pure and simple, and had organised them into a new and on the whole—speaking broadly—reformed and submissive bureaucracy, through which the new-model papacy transacted a new mass of counter-reformation business.

The attack on the accumulation by the cardinals of bishoprics, benefices and commendams had been part of the conciliarist attack on the whole curial system. Schemes had also been put forward at that time for making the cardinals officially and adequately representative of the various nations (even by having them nationally elected!) and for enhancing their position in the Church by reducing their numbers. This inevitably raised the whole fundamental question of their basic status, and whether their acknowledged right of electing the Pope and of acting as his advisers denoted some place *jure divino* in the hierarchy of the Church. Did they in fact not merely advise the Pope but actually cooperate in the papal government by virtue of some intrinsic status of their own within the 'corporation' of the Roman Church? Did they share, in their own right, in the divinely appointed powers of the Roman Church? Were they part of the 'corporation' of the Roman Church in the sense of being part of the papacy? Such a position had never been claimed —I believe—even by the canons of St John Lateran, the cathedral church of Rome. The point was argued to and fro in medieval controversy. Naturally its prominence and publicity were enhanced during the conciliar period, despite the academic nature of the argument. Under Eugenius IV, Nicholas V, Calixtus III and Pius II, the indirect pressure of conciliar opinion was still strong enough to ensure a more or less international college of cardinals, but a change set in with the Franciscan Sixtus IV, elected in 1471, with whom a new phase of the renaissance papacy may be said to have been inaugurated, and a large Italian majority of cardinals soon came into being. It was at the same period that the whole curia became more completely Italian and the layman, or married clerk in minor orders, less frequently found within its ranks. At the same time, with the full flowering of the High Renaissance, the social position of cardinals over bishops became more definite and pronounced, and the controversies over the corporate rights of the college, though continuous, were to some extent overshadowed by a renewed wave of criticism directed against their mode of life, their luxury and display, their accumulation of bishoprics and other benefices, and in many cases the political nature of their allegiances and actions. Non-resident cardinals like Wolsey in England, d'Amboise in France and others elsewhere were statesmen pure and simple; but the same charge was not incapable of being levelled at some of the members of the college resident in Rome. The 'reform' of the cardinals, in all these matters, became one of the cries of the hour and it is interesting that one of the most drastic programmes for effecting it is to be found in an unpublished bull of reform of Alexander VI which has been studied in an article by M. Célier, the historian of the datary, and which reveals the existence of extreme views on reform among certain cardinals and officials of that pontificate.[1] The proposals of the Lateran Council, where the bishops fought a losing battle against the cardinals on the one hand and the exempt orders on the other, were milder and, lacking executive sanction, ineffective. But, as with so much else, the Protestant revolution gave new edge to the movement for the reform of the cardinals and brought new factors into it. The new urgency to ensure the residence of bishops and other ecclesiastical officials in their sees now made the accumulation of sees and benefices, especially outside Italy, by absentee cardinals living mainly in Rome more and more reprehensible. Yet the enforcement of residence in Rome for cardinals was the answer of conservatives to the more radical plan of their residence in their bishoprics! Utopian proposals were, however, also in the air. An unknown memorialist under Clement VII suggested that each Pope appoint his own cardinals as an ecclesiastical senate of mixed lay and ecclesiastical composition, that the appointments should lapse on the Pope's death, and that the new Pope should be elected by an international body of bishops chosen by lot. This proposal struck at the heart of the main prerogative of the cardinals—to elect the Pope. But it served to make the point that, though the cardinals might elect the Pope, their whole position, indeed their whole being, depended on the papacy. The *Consilium de Emendanda Ecclesia* of 1537 concentrated on two practical aspects of cardinalitial reform: first, the disentanglement of the cardinals living in Rome from non-Italian bishoprics and benefices and the general reform of their manner of life and accumulation of ecclesiastical wealth; and, secondly, the reconstitution of the cardinals as an official ecclesiastical senate of papal advisers free from political considerations or controls, with a few non-Italians living abroad to maintain useful contacts. It is these two principles which underlie the development undergone by the cardinals in the sixteenth century and which form the basis of the position of the cardinals in the modern Church.

The moral reform and the political evolution of the college

[1] L. Célier, 'Alexandre VI et la réforme de l'Eglise', *Mélanges d'archéologie et d'histoire* (Ecole française de Rome), XXVII (1907), 65–124.

of cardinals during the Counter-Reformation proceeded hand in hand. They were accomplished under papal pressure and were marked by the silent dropping of claims both to the possession of independent powers *jure divino* and to rights of representation of nationalities. The Council of Trent indeed concerned itself with the reform of the cardinals and expressed a wish that they should be representatives of different nations. Its decrees stated that the cardinals were to be bound by the general regulations regarding residence, benefice-holding, clerical deportment and dress and so forth. These were valuable gestures—pious aspirations perhaps—but they exercised no influence on the development of the college from an institutional point of view, which the Pope kept entirely in his own hands.

The real transformation of the college of cardinals, both institutionally and morally, begins with Paul III, the aged renaissance pontiff who first gave direction and unity both to the Catholic reform and to the Counter-Reformation movement. Leo X had already considerably enlarged the college by his great creation, in 1517, of thirty-one new cardinals on one day, following on his discovery and punishment of a conspiracy against himself. This killed all chance of the reduction in numbers to twenty-four, or even twelve, which had been a corner-stone of most earlier reform proposals. Paul III, by his large creations, not only drove home the new practice of a college larger rather than smaller in numbers, but began its transformation as regards quality by introducing well-known reformers, some, like Contarini and Pole, laymen or in minor orders only. The presence among the cardinals of men such as Contarini, Carafa, Cervini, Pole, Morone, Sadoleto, Badia, Cortese and others was a portent and a turning-point. Henceforward, in place of a few isolated individuals, there would be a powerful reform party within the college, and a growing reform party, as the reform activity of the Popes increased and the climate of opinion gradually changed in the Holy City. At the same time the number of men among the cardinals to whom the Pope could turn for assured cooperation and genuine high-principled advice increased, and the formation of commissions or committees of cardinals for this or that piece of work

or to consider this or that reform, established a usage and a policy
that were to lead eventually to the new constitution of Sixtus V.

The years 1534–88 are thus the crucial ones in this moral and
institutional transformation of the cardinals and their work in
the Church. The numerous commissions and committees of
cardinals, with assistant advisers, which discussed the whole
range of ecclesiastical reform and in which the various parties,
from extreme rigorists to lenient traditionalists, set out their
views, were for the reform decrees of Trent what all the conferences on Justification were for doctrine: highly valuable preliminary clarifications and siftings of ideas and policies, and
their implications. Not only under Paul III, but also under
Julius III and Paul IV, the whole question of the status of the
cardinals, their wealth and their behaviour and their functions,
was discussed and thrashed out from every point of view, as one
aspect of the general problem of reform, while all the time in
practice conditions were getting a little better as the series of
papal bulls fulminated against the more reprehensible practices
of the unreformed. Paul IV, who rejected the idea of a general
council, was the most severe reformer of the cardinals, driving
many of them out of Rome in despair at his rigour; but at the
same time he used them with increasing regularity as agents of
general reform and may perhaps have had at the back of his
mind some idea of creating a hierarchy of permanent administrative bodies such as Sixtus V afterwards brought into being. But
his fondness for his own worthless nephews was Paul's undoing
and belied his other acts. The reign ended in shame and disaster.
What would happen under the more accommodating Pius IV—
a Medici, even if a spurious one? In fact, after the tornado of
Carafa, the small breeze set in again towards further reform,
perhaps a little unsteadily at times, but in the end with certainty
of direction. In addition to completing the Council of Trent—
a major diplomatic achievement—Pius IV saw to it that genuine
reformers continued to enter the Sacred College. To the already
established permanent committee, or board, of cardinals set over
the Roman inquisition by Paul III, he added a special committee
to deal with matters arising out of the Council of Trent (a sure

indication of the papal supremacy over the council), and his successors Pius V and Gregory XIII added others, notably one for the affairs of Germany. At the time of the completion of the Council of Trent, the transformation of the cardinals was therefore only at a half-way stage. The impetus which the council gave both to moral reform and to the accession of new work for the papacy completed the process. In the Rome of the Franciscan Sixtus V, who systematised the new specialised employment of the cardinals in small committees, Theatines and Jesuits and Capuchins and above all St Philip Neri had worked a wide moral regeneration of which historians cannot ignore the reality though they may questioningly scrutinise its extent; and a supply of active and eager men of a new generation was to hand for the staffing of the congregations of cardinals and for that of the tribunals and offices of the curia, men in whose lives the new spirituality of the Counter-Reformation was a living force. It would of course be absurd to represent Rome in 1588 as a city of saints. Many grave moral abuses and ills still remained. It would be equally absurd to fail to recognise the enormous change since 1527. The inspired work of saints and the laborious efforts of Popes had completed what the shock of the sack of 1527 had begun.

Sixtus V, in the bull *Immensa Dei*, dated 22 January 1588, set up for the Church an organised constitution of committees, or boards, of cardinals called 'congregations'.[1] These in some sense paralleled the less closely defined system of government by councils which the western monarchs were developing, and to which they had been driven by the same basic urges and necessities: the need for more efficient treatment of new ranges of business by dependent officials. If Sixtus V's constitution was more cut-and-dried than that of Elizabeth or Philip II, it was because his own sovereign position was clearer. Sixtus put a ceiling of seventy on the numbers of the sacred college. He laid down that there should be no more examples of brothers in it, and that at least four members should be doctors of theology, and he established fifteen specialised congregations, each of three

[1] Pastor, *History of the Popes*, XXI (1932), 245 ff.

to five cardinals with appropriate advisers and consultors. These were to help the Pope in the government of the Church from every point of view, from matters like the Inquisition, the interpretation of the decrees of the Council of Trent, the appointment of bishops or the affairs of the oriental Churches under Rome, down to the upkeep and administration of St Peter's, the care of the Vatican press, and the secular administration of the papal states, which under Sixtus V was becoming the main basis of papal finance—though Sixtus's own part in establishing order and security has perhaps been exaggerated. It would be tedious to enumerate in detail the congregations, which, with some changes and in cooperation with the older curial bodies, have continued to form the main framework of the central administration of the Roman Catholic Church ever since. It was the beginning of a more modern bureaucracy, in which the cardinals, tamed in temper, much reformed in morals, and transformed into a new officialdom from a turbulent and restless aristocracy, were at last able to fulfil their ambitions of the conciliar period in becoming intimately associated with the government of the Church, though denied their theoretical claims to possess *jure divino* a part of the substance of the rights of the Roman Church. They were the agents, not the sharers, of sovereignty. Unlike the older medieval organs of the curia which had grown up without conscious plan or design, the scope and competence of the congregations were formally set out in a sovereign act of creation. The full weekly consistory of all the cardinals in Rome continued to be held, but its functions tended to become more and more formal. The congregation system made it easier for the Pope to overcome opposition, although the medieval tradition of plain speaking, even to the Pope himself, was still far from dead, and cardinals of the old type, political and social, continued to exist up to the end of the *ancien régime*, if not beyond.

The congregational organisation fulfilled one great administrative need of the new papacy: it gave it a power of dealing efficiently and systematically and with reasonable swiftness with a large body of varied business, much of it new: whether it were the revision of the Vulgate, the interpretation of Trent's decrees, the affairs of the oriental Churches under its rule, the repair of St Peter's, or the functioning of the Holy Office. And it did all this not at any expense of the papal supremacy but by virtue of it, and in a way which converted previous competitors for a share in the actual ownership of papal power—the cardinals—into mere conveyors and dispensers of it. But there remained one other administrative necessity which the sixteenth-century papacy felt equally with other governing institutions of the day: the need for a more private and less formal kind of secretarial assistance than could be provided by any of the somewhat ossified medieval secretariats working to rigid forms of procedure. Like the king's court and the king's household in England, the papal court and the papal household, too, were inexhaustible sources of new administrative helps; and private personal assistants could be brought forward to do work in a more intimate and confidential way than was possible through the clerks either in the chancery or elsewhere. From certain arrangements made by Innocent VIII in 1488 among his clerks, exactly a hundred years before Sixtus V's bull establishing the congregations, there developed a personage, a chief clerk or private secretary, who came within a hundred years to wield very great power and to be intimately associated with the papal prime minister, the papal secretary of state.[1] The whole evolution of this person and his functions was much more rapid than the rise to political supremacy of the secretaries of state in England. But the office and its development seem essentially similar.

There are, however, a number of obscurities regarding the early history of the papal private secretary and of the secretary of state. And they are not all resolved by the account of the rise of the private secretary from the time of Martin V written in 1574 by Giovanni Carga, who had served under Tolomeo Gallio, the cardinal of Como, secretary of state to Gregory XIII. It would seem that, between them, first Leo X and then Paul III were responsible for separating the organisation of the private secretariat from the chancery, the latter Pope putting the new organ at the disposal of his grandson Alexander Farnese, whom he

[1] See Postscript, pp. 144 f.

trained to act as his chief adviser. The private secretary required two fundamental qualifications: good practical judgment, and a confessor-like capacity for keeping secrets. He also needed to know languages, be able to manage cyphers, have powers of drafting and composition, some knowledge of history and politics, and some power of managing subordinates without himself intruding upon the province of his superiors. He worked hand in hand with the cardinal most intimate with the Pope, and the exact delimitation of their spheres seems to have varied. According to Carga, the cardinal of Como under Gregory XIII not only had the general political supervision befitting a cardinal adviser but also himself performed the actual work of the *secretario intimo*. And if it were objected that such work was beneath the dignity of a cardinal, the answer, says Carga, is that 'the Pope wishes it so'. The private secretary enjoyed in the middle sixteenth century a modest salary in return for his heavy confidential labours, but benefices of one sort or another often came his way, and he might frequently rise to become a prelate and eventually even a cardinal. From Martin V onwards many Popes had tended to put their chief trust in members of their own family raised to the cardinalate, and from the confluence of this practice with the rise of the private secretary there emerged the finished product of the papal secretariat of state, usually presided over by a cardinal nephew. The desire of Popes to employ blood-relations in this high office proceeded not only out of family or personal affection. It was a way of being assured of loyalty and confidence and intimacy in an age when the modern spirit of public service with all its traditions and integrities had hardly come into existence in the higher ranks of any government service. For a century or more the cardinal nephew was an accepted institution, and showed to the world how personal an affair the papal monarchy still was in feeling, despite its vast expansion in extent, just as monarchy in England or France or Spain still retained its personal nature. The cardinal nephews were often men of surprising ability. One, Carlo Borromeo, was a saint. And it is worthy of remembrance that if some papal relatives promoted to the cardinalate in the sixteenth and seventeenth centuries were worthless and scandalous—the Carafas, some of the Farneses, del Montes, d'Altemps and others—two of the most high-minded pontiffs of the sixteenth century, the Dominican Pius V and the Franciscan Sixtus V, found themselves forced in the end, against their original principle, to take one of their relatives into political employment and cover him with the red hat.

The reform of the cardinals, their organisation into administrative boards, the decline of the whole consistory and the rise of the cardinal nephew, secretary of state, and the private secretariat, put an end to any project for regarding the college of cardinals as an international senate in which all nations should be represented. But the relations between the papacy and the nations and other states of Europe certainly presented profound problems for the Counter-Reformation: speculative problems of theoretical competence as between Church and state, functional problems of everyday relationships.

In certain respects the Catholic secular powers had it in their hands to make or mar the Counter-Reformation. It was a task of the utmost importance to persuade them to accept and promote the disciplinary decrees of Trent and, if possible, to have these incorporated as part and parcel of the law of the land. Few, if any, did this without exception. In France, it was never done. It was, I think, first and foremost the necessity of obtaining the support of the state, first for the convocation and progress of the Council of Trent, and then for the enforcement of the Tridentine decrees of reform, that developed the diplomatic system of resident papal nuncios for the secular powers finally organised and established as permanent by Gregory XIII.

Ever since the fifteenth century had witnessed the beginnings of modern diplomacy, papal representatives at secular courts had been prominent among those who had done much to develop it. The progress both of the Reformation and of the Counter-Reformation had multiplied the necessity for frequent missions of personages from Rome. The title of legate was usually reserved for either those with high personal status, such as that of a cardinal, or those whose mission was of outstanding importance.

Normally the term nuncio was employed, and institutionally the nuncios have a financial origin in that they descend from the resident papal tax-collectors who were often entrusted with business of other kinds. More and more, as the sixteenth century wore on, the papacy, like the other European powers, found it essential to have permanent representatives at other courts, to give them information, and to form permanent channels of communication. It was Gregory XIII, the predecessor of Sixtus V, who reorganised and expanded into a permanent established system the growing practice of permanent resident papal nuncios accredited to the secular powers as diplomatic representatives. The title of legate either became purely honorific in certain archbishops or was reserved for those cardinals sent on occasional *ad hoc* missions of outstanding importance. The nuncios quickly became the vital links between the counter-reformation papacy in Rome and the progress of the Counter-Reformation outside Rome, and their extreme importance in the history of Catholicism at this period is now winning increasing recognition. Their functions were an amalgam of the political and the ecclesiastical. Primarily diplomatic agents, they had to urge the secular powers to support the new reforms, to take up the fight against Protestantism as vigorously as possible, and on the whole to follow the line of policy desired by Rome. They were also empowered to act as direct ecclesiastical agents: to concern themselves with the direct promotion through the local hierarchies of reform in the clergy and in the laity, of the establishment of seminaries and so forth, and with the importation of the new Roman spirit. That is to say, they were often both diplomats accredited to the state and direct ecclesiastical agents of the Pope in respect of the Church, links between the Pope and the bishops. Their office and their work did much to push forward the direct papal control over the life of the western Catholic Church. Gregory XIII chose his men with care. Himself a canonist, he selected as his agents men who had grown up in the service of the judicial departments of the curia. But though not considered in Rome to be one of the extreme reformers—indeed he was regarded as a definite reaction from his predecessor, the later canonised Dominican Pope Pius V—Gregory nonetheless chose men associated also with the new fervour and spiritual disciplines, as well as men endowed with skill, culture and integrity. The nuncios were usually made bishops or archbishops with titles *in partibus infidelium* and were paid regular salaries. They were, in fact, part of the new ecclesiastical officialdom elaborated by the counter-reformation papacy on more up-to-date lines. These men performed services to the Counter-Reformation which can hardly be exaggerated. Not all of them, naturally, were successful: sometimes their task was in itself too difficult; sometimes their abilities or character fell short. But by and large they did extremely valuable work and set up a new and more satisfactory link between the papacy and the Catholic states. The late Dr Kidd, who had plainly read his Pastor on this matter, paid a high tribute to the nuncios and their work in his, in many other ways very unsatisfactory, book on the Counter-Reformation.[1] Looked at from another point of view the papal nuncios were simply ecclesiastical examples of the general development of a system of permanent ambassadors between the European states. And again, in this instance of correlation of method between Church and state, a certain primacy was conceded to the Church by the papal nuncio becoming everywhere recognised as doyen of the diplomatic corps.

At the beginning of Gregory XIII's pontificate, nuncios already existed in Venice, Turin, Florence and Naples; in Spain, Portugal, France and Poland; and there was one at the imperial court in Germany. Numerically and geographically the expansion under Gregory XIII was chiefly in Germany, where the seventies and eighties of the century saw the turn of the tide and the real beginning of the Catholic Reformation and the Counter-Reformation on an important scale. A decade or more after the conclusion of the Council of Trent, its effects began to be felt in the Germanic territories, in conjunction with the work of the Jesuits and the gradual revival of spirit and energy among the

[1] B. J. Kidd, *The Counter-Reformation* (London, 1933), p. 260; the subject is also discussed in G. Alberigo, 'Diplomazia e vita della Chiesa nel xvi secolo', *Critica storica* (Florence), I (1962), 49-69, which I have not seen.

members of the German episcopate. Gregory XIII's policy of establishing national colleges in Rome for the education of clergy also brought much fruit, and the German College in Rome, under Jesuit management, was an important factor in the revival of German Catholicism. One great hindrance in Germany itself was the tremendous size of the wealthy dioceses compared with the smaller, in some instances indeed minute, and poverty-stricken Italian ones. But a redivision of dioceses in Germany was far too radical an idea to enter into any sixteenth-century head. Gregory XIII not only established a permanent nuncio in Switzerland; he also established, under the direction of the main German nuncio at the imperial court, other technically independent nuncios at Salzburg and at Cologne, and in Bavaria and Styria. The nuncio at Cologne had charge of the affairs of the Catholics in Holland; his brother in Brussels looked after the affairs of the Catholics in England. Catholic minorities elsewhere were similarly placed under nuncios. The pattern of the nunciatures rivalled in importance that of the hierarchy itself.

The failure to consider a multiplication or redivision of dioceses in Germany is certainly one sign of the essentially conservative nature of the Catholic reform in regard to the preservation of the existing ecclesiastical organisation. But in new mission lands where there had been no dioceses before, or in lands where the Catholic organisation had been destroyed, the problem was different. Here were two tasks that called for novelty of approach. The Counter-Reformation had not only Europe but also a wider world to consider; its missionary programme was vast throughout the sixteenth and seventeenth centuries, and if the expansion of Europe is one of the most important events of the post-medieval epoch in history, the expansion of Catholicism outside Europe surely goes closely with it. It was perhaps in this sphere that true originality and enterprise found their most congenial spheres within the counter-reformation Church. It must never be forgotten that the conversion of the infidel or the heathen was one of the original driving motives of St Ignatius, and that the missionary work which took his sons all over the globe, following in the wake of the early missionaries who had accompanied the first Iberian expansions, has never ceased from that day to this to hold a very high place in the programme and in the self-consciousness of the Society of Jesus. Indeed it was Rome, rather than Geneva or Wittenberg or Canterbury, which was first able to spread Christianity into the newly discovered lands. While Rome was beginning to lose Germany and Switzerland and Scandinavia, she was simultaneously planting her hierarchies in Mexico and Peru and central America. The Jesuits were in Brazil in the 1550s, and the meteoric career of Francis Xavier in the Far East had closed long before Parsons and Campion landed in England. In nothing else, perhaps, is the forceful vigour of the revived Catholicism of the sixteenth century seen to better advantage than in this far-flung missionary enterprise, which raised problems of such outstanding difficulty in the spiritual as well as in the material sphere. In the western hemisphere and in central Africa extraordinary novelties confronted the missionary in the character and condition of the American and African natives; in the sophisticated East, however, the missionaries, not associated so completely, or so universally, with territorial political conquest, came up against old-established philosophies. While the Catholic spiritual conquests in the East cannot be said to have been, on any large scale, either lasting or significant, it was not perhaps until the very end of the seventeenth century that the predominance of the Protestant and Anglo-Saxon elements on the North American continent began to seem at all possible. In a geographical sense, if in no other, Catholicism had called in new worlds to redress the balance of the old.

It is, perhaps, surprising that it was not until 1622 that a special congregation of cardinals, the famous *Congregatio de Propaganda Fide*, was instituted, during the short pontificate of Gregory XV, to have the care and oversight of all the missions.[1] It had indeed been foreshadowed by earlier organisations set up by Pius V, Gregory XIII and Clement VIII (1592–1605). But not even Sixtus V in his great constituent act of 1588 had included a special congregation for the missions among his newly organised bodies. The establishment of a permanent congrega-

---

[1] Pastor, *History of the Popes*, XXVII (1938), 129 ff.; see Postscript, pp. 137, 140 f.

tion had for several years before 1622 been urged by various missionaries, especially by certain Carmelite and Capuchin friars who had worked in the East. The *Congregatio de Propaganda Fide* had a special character of its own. It comprised no fewer than thirteen cardinals (the normal number in a congregation was about five or six) with various bishops and a very active first secretary. It was given very full powers and ample financial resources, and it was allowed many of its necessary secretarial functions and postal necessities free of charge. It was entrusted not only with the mission field in America, Asia and Africa—a vast enough commitment in itself—but also with the oriental bodies under Rome: Maronites, Ruthenians of the 1595 Union in Poland, Catholic Armenians and others; it supervised the Catholic minorities in all parts of Europe where the hierarchy in submission to Rome no longer existed—England, Scotland, Holland, Scandinavia—and also in places like the Balkans, Greece, Cyprus, Crete, the Levant, where united and non-united oriental Churches were curiously and confusingly mixed up.

The principal aim of this pontifical ministry of missions, carrying the direct and immediate jurisdictional power of Rome over so wide an area, was to give uniform religious character to all the missions and to bind them closely to the authority of Rome: to supervise all the problems concerning literature, controversial methods, institution of colleges, methods of propaganda, the training of native clergy where this was undertaken—all the prodigious activities of an intellectual, financial and administrative kind which the whole work involved. Secondly, and very importantly, it was the task of *Propaganda* to loosen the ever-tightening hand of the colonising powers over missionary activities in their colonial areas, and this meant, in practice, chiefly opposing the direct interference of the Portuguese and Spanish governments in the religious side of the missions. This was a very powerful factor behind the foundation of *Propaganda*. Behind *Propaganda* lay a new extension of missionary urge based on the Mediterranean and French culture of the early seventeenth century, together with a re-emergence in the mission fields of the chronic conflicts between Church and state over religious and ecclesiastical policy. Rome's aim in 1622 was to free the missions from state control.[1]

I have now come very near the end of my time—if, indeed, I have not already gone beyond it. But before concluding, I feel that it would not be inappropriate for me to recall what I said at the outset about what has been, and what has not been, my aim in this course. I have not tried to give anything in the nature of a complete summary of the Counter-Reformation or to pass a final judgment. That, I think, would be beyond my powers, and would involve the integration into the picture of many factors on which I have not touched. I do not intend to attempt it now at the eleventh hour. I have, however, attempted to convey my view that in the Counter-Reformation we have to do with something much larger, much more complex in nature and origin, than a mere conservative reaction to the Protestant challenge in the sphere of religion; and that we must find a more comprehensive formula in which to grasp the whole historical significance of the birth-pangs of modern Catholicism, under the Roman headship, as the medieval Church and medieval religion, forcibly deprived of their medieval monopoly, adapted themselves under the pressure of unwelcome circumstances to the strange conditions of post-medieval society and to the permanent presence in the world of competitors claiming Christian truth in other forms. The reinvigoration of the religious urge which was part and parcel of the new vigour of European life in the sixteenth century ay behind the Catholic revival and the Counter-Reformation as it ay behind the successes of Luther and Calvin. While no Christian body of the name could swallow *in toto* the purely humanistic attitude to life, assimilable elements of humanism in some quantity entered into the make-up of counter-reformation religion, in its new individualism of spirituality and spiritual discipline, in its theological presupposition regarding free will, in some aspects of its literature, in much of its educational method.

It is true that, in the shock of having to contend against successful opposition to her conception of Christian truth—

---

[1] But compare the remark of Rogier cited below, Postscript, p. 141, n. 2.

opposition supported, furthermore, in many places by the state—counter-reformation Catholicism, forced on to a desperate defensive, turned at times a somewhat prejudiced eye upon the enlargements of the mind's horizon which were gradually being effected in the world of intellectual speculation, and turned wholeheartedly for help in her peril to the methods of force and constraint. If I have not dwelt upon the theme of persecution, it is not because I am unaware of it or would wish to minimise either its reality or its significance. All that is sufficiently well known. The issue of freedom of personal belief is one of the deepest in human history. But the employment of force, the recourse to persecution and the methods of inquisition by both Church and state in counter-reformation Catholicism are not in themselves wholly out of keeping with the sixteenth-century mentality in general, and do not, I would claim, invalidate my two main theses. They are: first, that what is conventionally called the Counter-Reformation was fundamentally a powerful revival of religion and should be studied as such; and, secondly, that the methods which the Counter-Reformation devised, both spiritually and institutionally, in order to reconstitute and reinvigorate Catholicism and to set it up on its new course in the modern world with new powers and new organs, under papal guidance and control, and drawing for the time its immediate and main practical strength from the resources of the Mediterranean and French civilisation of the sixteenth and seventeenth centuries—that all these methods reveal a remarkable degree of accord with the general spirit and the general methods of their times. My aim in these lectures has been to explore, as objectively as my own personal convictions permit me to do, one or two avenues of approach of this nature—and no doubt there are others as well—along which it seems to me that the way lies to a fuller understanding of all that is involved for European history in the Counter-Reformation defined in the widest sense.

*Cambridge, 1951*

# EDITOR'S POSTSCRIPT

I have written this postscript in order to convey some idea of what has been going on in the study of the Counter-Reformation in the fifteen years since Evennett wrote, and to discuss some aspects of its history on which he had comparatively little to say. I could not in any case claim to be representing his views, but I should perhaps explain that I have taken the opportunity to pursue, *à propos* of such of the more recent work as I have read and found illuminating, thoughts that started when my own special preoccupations were confronted with what I believe to be the first serious attempt at a general understanding of the subject ever made by an English historian. I do not apologise for the fact that these preoccupations concern the history of English Catholicism: it is after all surely rather odd that Evennett should have devoted so little attention to English problems, and I would hope in redressing the balance, even in over-redressing it, to be following as freely as he would have expected the inspiration he wished to give.

Ignatius and his *Spiritual Exercises* were, for Evennett, the heart of the matter. How securely, one may ask, does his view of them stand after fifteen years? Two questions arise, one about the sources of the *Exercises*, another about the spirit which they express and encourage. There has been some dispute over the first of these: Evennett came down carefully but rather firmly in favour of taking them as a culmination of the northern *devotio moderna* tradition; on the other hand the Austrian Jesuits Hugo and Karl Rahner have denied that this movement had any serious influence on Ignatius, and Hugo Rahner has written of a 'radical distinction' between the two spiritualities.[1] Their criticism seems largley inspired by the desire to safeguard spiritual experience as

---

[1] H. Rahner, *The spirituality of St Ignatius Loyola* (Westminster, Md., 1953: English translation of *Ignatius von Loyola und das geschichtliche Werden seiner Frömmigkeit*, Vienna, 1947), p. 55; K. Rahner, *The dynamic element in the Church* (Freiburg/London, 1964), pp. 84–170, esp. pp. 86 f.

a region of certainty transcending any historical or psychological conditions, and a historian may think twice before commenting on it. But, faced with Karl Rahner's assurance that Ignatius really belongs not to his own time but to an archaic past or an unrevealed future, he is bound to feel uneasy. Evennett seems to have expressed his discomfort by dropping Hugo Rahner from his team of Jesuit scholars who have grappled with the 'problem of envisaging St Ignatius in his historical setting'; his 'Was it *all* infused at Manresa?' looks as if it was meant as a polite rejection of the Rahnerian view.[1] He believed that the chief agent for the transmission to Ignatius of the *devotio moderna* was the Benedictine order, and the prevailing view would now seem to be that this communication occurred, not only through a direct contact with the school of Cisneros at Montserrat, but also by a broader if more roundabout route through northern Italy and the individualist monasticism of Santa Justina.[2] Given the pattern of Iberian relations with the rest of Europe during the sixteenth century, this seems entirely plausible. But support for the general point has also come from an unexpected quarter. Discussing the spiritual sector of English 'metaphysical' poetry of the earlier seventeenth century in his *The Poetry of Meditation*,[3] Professor Louis L. Martz has found the key to its peculiar character in its adherence to a single, though diverse, meditative tradition in which Mombaer, the *Spiritual Exercises* and their Jesuit commentators figure with St François de Sales and others in a harmony which seems more fundamental than Jesuit commentators are at present willing to allow.[4] There is no question of treating Ignatius as a

---

[1] See above, pp. 55–6; cf. J. de Guibert, *La spiritualité de la Compagnie de Jésus*, p. 104, n. 17.
[2] Albareda, 'Intorno alla scuola...' (above, p. 35, n. 2), p. 299; cf. Leturia, *art. cit.* above, p. 59 n., and L. Cognet, *Post-Reformation spirituality* (London, 1959: English translation of *De la dévotion moderne à la spiritualité française*, Paris, 1958), pp. 10 f.; E. Delaruelle, E.-R. Lebande, P. Ourliac, *L'Eglise au temps du Grand Schisme et de la crise conciliaire*, II (Fliche and Martin, *Histoire de l'Eglise*, XIV, part 2, *s.l.*, 1964), 1047 f., 938 f.
[3] *Yale Studies in English*, CXXV (New Haven/London, 1954).
[4] Thus I. Iparraguirre, *Introduzione allo studio degli Esercizi Spirituali di San Ignazio* (Rome, 1951), p. 6: 'Tutte queste dipendenze non sorpassano la superficie del libro...'; but cf. the very favourable remarks on Mombaer by the sixteenth-century Jesuit Antonio Possevino, in Watrigant, 'La méditation méthodique et Jean Mauburnus' (above, p. 32 n.), p. 14.

simple follower of Groote, or Groote as a simple precursor of Ignatius, and it is possible that Evennett later felt that he had in 1951 somewhat overemphasised the dependence.[1] Concentration on the *Spiritual Exercises* may obscure the fact that its meditative techniques were primarily meant to serve in special situations and for special problems, and not to provide a whole pattern of life. But this is equally true of the Brothers of the Common Life;[2] and, considering the undoubted common ground in Thomas à Kempis, it seems reasonable to believe that Ignatius received from the north a model of intensely cultivated inwardness which he adapted to, but which also helped him to clarify, his own more widely practical intentions.

The point is important because it evokes, without of course exhausting, the crucial suggestion that Ignatius ought to be considered as embracing rather than fighting the general tendencies of his age. Two features of Ignatian spirituality, for Evennett, argued for this conformity: its individualism and its activism. I do not think there would now be much informed disagreement on either of these points. The society itself seems to be finding that its own period of nineteenth-century restoration manifested a rigidity and a literalism hardly in keeping with Ignatius's original thought,[3] and recent work has emphasised how radical an activism the early Jesuits professed. Circumstances have here helped understanding. Much of the history of the French Church, and indeed of France, during the twentieth century lies between Bremond's uncomprehending 'critique de l'oraison pratique',[4] published in 1928, and some of the essays

[1] I gather this from some phrases in his broadcast talk, 'The Counter-Reformation', in J. Hurstfield (ed.), *The Reformation crisis*, pp. 66 f.

[2] Post, *De moderne devotie*, pp. 136–9; cf. the quotations from Mombaer, etc., in Watrigant, 'La méditation méthodique et l'école des Frères de la Vie Commune' (above, p. 32 n.), pp. 153–5.

[3] Thus Iparraguirre, *op. cit.* p. 27, where he remarks that the profitable use of the *Exercises* depends on the extent to which they call on the individual experience of the director as well as on that of the exercitant, and implies that directors have not always grasped the point. Some observations of Pope Paul VI in his speech to the Jesuit general congregation, 16 November 1966 (*Civiltà Cattolica*, 3 December 1966, p. 494), seem relevant.

[4] H. Bremond, *Histoire littéraire du sentiment religieux*, VIII, 261 ff. The exact title of Bremond's book deserves perhaps more notice than it has received.

in Jesuit spirituality contributed to the review *Christus* during the 1950s. Among these I think Evennett would have felt most sympathetic to Fr Maurice Giuliani's 'Finding God in All Things', which presents with rare simplicity the idea that for Ignatius and his followers 'devotion', and indeed prayer, was not to be thought of as a distinct type of activity, but as a possible tone of all activity.[1] The recent history of Germany has proved a less fruitful environment, and Hugo Rahner's response to it seems, by comparison with Giuliani's, a little crude. Anyone who insists, in 1947, on the military and chivalric nature of Ignatian spirituality lays himself open to a charge of promoting the anti-Bolshevik crusade in defiance of the almost unanimous opinion of modern scholars:[2] to which I would add for myself that in circumstances where, if in any, the terminology of warfare might with reason have suggested itself, the English Jesuits spoke of themselves equally often as engaged in a *negotium* as in a *bellum*.[3] Rahner has in any event made it perfectly clear that a preoccupation with the aftermath of Nazism lies behind his anxiety to rehabilitate ideals of service and obedience through the claim that the only object of true service is the Church.[4] Active apostolicity, in his view, was for Ignatius immediately and essentially ecclesiastical: in the vision at Manresa he became at once apostle and churchman, abandoning the individualism which his earlier and more romantic conception of service had implied, and so establishing his radical divergence from the unecclesiastical, and therefore catastrophically misguided, devotion of the north.[5] That this was a view governed far too closely by the considerations of the moment seems to have been

---

[1] *Finding God in all things: essays in Jesuit spirituality selected from* Christus (tr. Wm. J. Young, Chicago, 1958), pp. 3–24; the review began to appear in Paris in 1953. See also Iparraguirre's commentary on the 'Contemplation for Obtaining Love', *Introduzione*, pp. 84–92, and commentators, especially Gagliardi, there cited; and Guibert, *La spiritualité de la Compagnie de Jésus*, pp. 192 f.

[2] Examples above, p. 62, n. 1.

[3] In six cases from Robert Parsons's letters between 1580 and 1584 the terms used are 'hanc pugnam', 'universa (ut ita loquar) mercatura nostra', 'negotiis nostris', 'hujus belli nostri', 'hujus belli spiritualis', 'huic sancto negotio' (Catholic Record Society, XXXIX (1942), 55, 73, 106, 131, 229, 262); the correspondents are Agazzari, rector of the English College in Rome, Acquaviva and Ribadeneira.

[4] H. Rahner (see p. 126 n.), pp. vi–vii, 20, 80, 112.    [5] *Ibid.* pp. 55 f.

recognised by Karl Rahner, whose more recent discussion treats this point rather differently.[1]

Evennett's account of Ignatius's progress is here, I think, specially valuable. It is above all an evolutionary account, seeking to do justice to every aspect of his final achievement as the outcome of a developing experience. Where Hugo Rahner has seen him become in a flash, at a trumpet-crash, both apostle and churchman, Evennett speaks of him, after Manresa, as now the 'incipient apostle', with the society 'in principle conceived', and after Paris as 'becoming'—the emphasis is on the process rather than on the result—'a churchman as well as an apostle'.[2] This again is a point of some consequence: the question raised is whether we are to regard as a structural pillar of the Ignatian building the belief that God is best served in the free and full activity of the individual. Of course Ignatius believed, and perhaps more strongly as his spiritual education proceeded, that a pure activism was as open to spurious as to genuine inspiration. But I doubt if one can do justice to the special character of his ideal, or to the special problems which it created, unless one agrees, more or less, with Giuliani that for him the dangers of activity were not to be avoided by prior decisions, and in a sense not to be avoided at all, but only kept up with by a continuous internal mechanism of self-examination and mortification.[3] Those who felt that there was kinship between him and Machiavelli may, in this respect, have had some truth on their side; both were surely casualties or beneficiaries of the disintegration of scholastic ethics. Ignatius's, I would suggest, was an ideal which demanded almost as much of the hierarchical Church as it conceded to it, and no interpretation of it will do which makes too little room for the dialectics of obedience and initiative. Few religious superiors can have told members of their order so firmly to forget the rules and do what they thought best.[4]

---

[1] *The dynamic element in the Church*, p. 93, etc.
[2] See above, pp. 60–1.
[3] 'Finding God in all things', pp. 19 f. Similarly, on this point, Karl Rahner, *op. cit.* p. 110: 'Ignatius tacitly presupposes a philosophy of human existence in which a moral decision in its individuality is not merely an instance of general ethical principles.'
[4] See especially his instructions to Oliver Manare in Guibert, *op. cit.* p. 89.

An intuition of the power of human action, and anxiety to release this power for the pursuit of divine enterprises, were surely, if not *sub specie aeternitatis* the most important, at least historically the most distinctive features of Ignatius's spirituality. Its general conformity with the tendencies of his age seems perfectly obvious, though it would be helpful if this could be shown in a wider variety of precisely determined fields than seem so far to have been investigated. As an example, I would offer the suggestion that Elizabethan Catholicism should be read as an activism which the Jesuits did not at all invent but which recognised in the Jesuit ideal the clearest model of what it had in mind.[1] This may seem a parochial illustration. But in England anyway, as Martz has shown, confessional frontiers were no barrier to the diffusion of meditative practice; and Robert Parsons's explicitly anti-controversial manual of conversion, the *Book of Resolution*, was widely acceptable to Protestant fellow-countrymen as providing them with 'some one sufficient direction for matters of life and spirit'.[2] Nor need we think of these matters as excluding the more prosaic regions of behaviour. How far, after all, was the Ignatian idea from that intramundane asceticism in which Max Weber detected the source of a special Calvinist bent towards economic enterprise? For Weber, it was particular to Calvinist Christianity to recognise true faith in a type of behaviour which promoted within the world the visible glory of God, to call for the replacement of what he considered a Catholic diffusion of unrelated works by a life of systematically controlled and rationalised activity.[3] It is remarkable that while writing this celebrated passage, while indeed citing the formula *in majorem Dei gloriam*, he should apparently not have asked himself whether his description might not apply with equal

[1] John Bossy, 'The character of Elizabethan Catholicism', in *Past and Present*, no. 21 (1962), and T. Aston (ed.), *Crisis in Europe, 1560–1660* (London, 1965), pp. 223–46, esp. pp. 231 f. Some practical conditions and consequences of activism are investigated in 'Rome and the Elizabethan Catholics: a question of geography', *The Historical Journal*, VII (1964), 135–42.

[2] *The first booke of the Christian exercise, appertayning to resolution* ([Rouen,] 1582), preface, p. 2; Martz, *The poetry of meditation*, p. 8.

[3] *The Protestant ethic and the spirit of capitalism* (trans. Talcott Parsons, London, 1930), pp. 108–17.

felicity to Jesuits. Yet Richard Baxter, on whom Weber so largely drew, acknowledged that he owed his conversion to Parsons's book, and his *Christian Directory* seems visibly indebted to it for its title and general motive.[1] Each tradition, no doubt, bred its own variety of activism; but there seems little reason to quarrel with Professor Trevor-Roper's conclusion that what is at issue here is, broadly speaking, a supraconfessional doctrine of the sanctity of secular work.[2]

Several avenues of enquiry, pursued so far as I know without reference to one another or to the account of the subject presented above, seem therefore to converge upon a single prospect. The case for the modernity of the Jesuits, and for the Counter-Reformation as a process of modernisation, stands up, if anything, better in 1966 than it did in 1951. It contains nonetheless the serious difficulty that while it may account for the realities of 1550 or 1600 it will hardly do for those of 1700, still less of 1800. The case for associating the counter-reformation Church with reaction or sterility, economic, social, political and intellectual, remains in the long run very powerful, and no account of it should end without attempting a solution.

Evennett was in these lectures concerned to draw attention to the positive aspects of the Counter-Reformation, and did not here, or so far as I know anywhere, go very deeply into the question of its decline. Yet, by contrast with more traditional treatments, his own reading of the subject made this a peculiarly urgent problem. He did indeed suggest that this decline was connected with a crisis of Mediterranean civilisation, dating from the early seventeenth century, which had then been recently expounded by Braudel:[3] the idea, perhaps rather novel in 1951, seems now more like a commonplace. I should think it would be generally agreed that a shift of great importance occurred at this time;

---

[1] Helen C. White, *English devotional literature, 1600–1640* (Madison, Wisc., 1931), pp. 143 f.; G. F. Nuttall, *Richard Baxter* (London, 1965), pp. 12 f.; Weber, *The Protestant ethic*, pp. 158 f.

[2] H. R. Trevor-Roper, 'Religion, the Reformation and social change', in G. A. Hayes-McCoy (ed.), *Historical Studies* IV: *Papers read before the fifth Irish Conference of Historians* (London, 1963), pp. 18–44, esp. 35 f. and n. 35.

[3] See above, pp. 20 f.

that, to borrow a Braudelian metaphor, the centre of gravity of European society tipped over from a Mediterranean to an Atlantic and from an overwhelmingly Catholic to a predominantly Protestant location. The running-down of the Counter-Reformation may very properly be interpreted as a consequence of this shift on the spirit and structure of the Catholic Church; but it seems legitimate to point, as Trevor-Roper has done in the essay already cited, to the dangers of employing the idea in too mechanical a way, and so of neglecting social and institutional problems.[1] In itself the shift was a neutral phenomenon: the question is surely why there turned out to be no northern Catholicism, except possibly that of France, able to take the strain. This has been variously explained as a consequence of national or racial temper, of governmental repression, or of an inherent kinship between Protestantism and capitalism. But each of these explanations has come to look more and more unreliable as time has gone by, and this seems the moment to look for clues inside counter-reformation Catholicism itself.

Anyone who has read these lectures will have been surprised that Evennett found it possible to construct a convincing and at least reasonably comprehensive plan of the Counter-Reformation almost without mentioning the Council of Trent. This omission may not have been as important as it seems at first sight: Evennett may well have felt in 1951 that further thought about the council was best left until the completion of Jedin's *History*, then thought to be fairly imminent. But he must in any case have been less convinced than Jedin of the 'fact that a whole epoch of the Church has been fashioned by this Council',[2] and events seem to have justified his caution. Since then, Tridentine interpretation has gone into some kind of crisis:[3] Jedin's *History* is still no farther than 1547; and the work of M. Dupront of the Sorbonne and Professor Alberigo of Florence has implied a general revision of historical ideas about the council.

[1] *Art. cit.* pp. 18 f.
[2] H. Jedin, *Ecumenical councils of the Catholic Church* (Freiburg-im-B., etc., 1960), p. 186.
[3] Cf. G. Alberigo, 'The Council of Trent: new views on the occasion of its 4th centenary', *Concilium*, VII, no. 1 (Sept. 1965), 38–48.

For Dupront, Trent was an end, not a beginning—'le dernier des Conciles'.[1] As an institutional type, the council, like the crusade and perhaps also the notion of reform, was an organ of a solidary Christendom, and Trent retained this character of a collective occasion, intended to achieve in face-to-face communion a sacred purgation of the Church. The role which it actually played was something more like that played in the history of the French monarchy by the States General of 1614.[2] It announced with the solemnity which only a council could bestow that the days of Christendom, and therefore of councils, were over, and that in the future the destiny of the Church must lie with the two powers in which, like Evennett, Dupront sees the fuel and the engine of modern Catholicism: the spirituality of the modern devotion and the independent spiritual sovereignty of Rome. His remark that 'l'histoire du Concile de Trente est du patrimoine commun'[3] may not itself have been intended to mean that the council was an event in the general history of Christendom and not in the particular history of Catholicism; but this is the clear trend of his argument. It is surely defensible, not only in respect of the sociological fact of the council, but also in some degree of the debates which took place there. Jedin's *History* has already made it clear that, however much papal anxiety to conclude may have sharpened or hurried their dogmatic decisions, the range of opinion expressed by Tridentine theologians on scripture or Justification covered at one end almost the whole range of respectable Protestantism. It becomes more and more desirable to treat them as participants in a wider debate; and more and more difficult to see, for example, Seripando and his allies—'venus', says Dupront, 'trop tard ou bien trop tôt'[4]—

[1] A. Dupront, 'Du Concile de Trente: réflexions autour d'un iv[e] centenaire', *Revue historique*, CCVI (1951), 262–80; 'Le Concile de Trente', in B. Botte, etc., *Le Concile et les Conciles (s.l.,* 1960), pp. 202–43—the quotation is from p. 203 n.; *Les conciles de l'Eglise moderne et contemporaine* (Centre de Documentation Universitaire, Paris, 1963)—I have only seen the first part of this course of lectures, which covers roughly the same ground as Jedin's first volume. In Dupront's discussion the French connotations of 'moderne' should possibly be borne in mind.
[2] P. Blet, *Le clergé de France et la monarchie, 1615–1666* (2 vols., Rome, 1959), I, 122.
[3] 'Du Concile de Trente', p. 280; note the appreciative remarks in L. Just, 'Neue Arbeiten zur Gechichte des Konzils von Trient', *Archiv für Reformationsgeschichte*, XLIV (1953), 243.    [4] 'Le Concile de Trente', pp. 206 f.

as making any large contribution to the post-Tridentine Church. This difficulty has been increased by recent work on Pole's conduct in England, which has inspired the illuminating thought that Queen Mary 'failed to discover the Counter-Reformation'.[1]

There remains one large obstacle to accepting the excision of Trent from the Counter-Reformation: in its emphasis on the role of the bishop in the Church, Trent defined an ideal of great practical importance in the following centuries. The bitter battle over the theoretical aspects of this problem which occurred during the final sessions of the council has lately been re-examined by Alberigo;[2] and beneath an argument about the respective powers of bishops and Pope may be detected a more profound issue about the degree to which the institutional structure of the Church was open to change. For many of the fathers the hierarchical order which turned upon the bishops was in general and in detail divinely ordained, and they held almost without exception that what the Church needed was the restoration of a primitive and godly episcopate.[3] Some wished for the dogmatic definition of a point which the council's disciplinary decrees had in effect taken for granted. In the interventions of Ignatius's successor, Laínez, the incompatibility of even moderate expressions of this attitude with the activism of the Jesuits was argued with extreme clarity. Laínez has been most famous here for his rigorous and exhaustive distinction, in the episcopate, between the power of order and the power of jurisdiction, a distinction which, as Alberigo explains, had little of the traditional justification which he claimed for it. But his underlying motive, entirely coherent with what has been suggested of the whole Jesuit outlook, was clearly to reduce as far as possible the limits within which the structure of the Church should be considered as divinely ordained, and so make room for a degree of flexibility which would give the widest scope for exercising human initiative in a variable world. The lines of his argument will sound oddly familiar to historians of the Church of England. He held that nothing

---

[1] A. G. Dickens, *The English Reformation* (London, 1964), p. 280.

[2] G. Alberigo, *Lo sviluppo della dottrina sui poteri nella chiesa universale* (Rome/Freiburg, 1964).

[3] Earlier phases of the debate in Jedin, *History of the Council of Trent*, II, 317–69.

which did not depend on the direct word of God or on its immediate and rigorous consequences, no act or institution in which the intervention of generally human or specifically ecclesiastical creativity could be discerned, ought to be considered of divine ordinance. Thus, in so far as the sacrament of holy order was of immediate divine institution, bishops were *iure divino* in the Church to administer it; otherwise their general and particular powers were creations of human and ecclesiastical authority and so subject to indefinite mutation.[1] The rigour of Laínez's argument brought him in the end to what may be described as a papalist presbyterianism: 'bishops, according to Laínez, outside their sacramental powers, could not be said to be by divine right superior to other priests, were it not for the fact that the claim for a *iure divino* equality of all priests would be heretical because it excluded the *iure divino* superiority of the Pope'.[2] This reminds one of Cardinal Manning's remark, frequently anticipated in the sixteenth and seventeenth centuries and apparently inspired by a look into the archives of his archbishopric, that the Pope was the only plank between a Jesuit and a Presbyterian. As an attempt to detach the Church from its inherited beneficial structure and so make its human and material resources more immediately available where they might be used most efficiently, Laínez's thesis was found 'extremely displeasing' by the bishops of whom the council was composed.[3] Its implied programme of activity was clearly much at odds with the episcopally directed reform which the fathers were attempting to promote. But one wonders whether his principles were so essentially papalist as the opposition felt, and whether he was not practising, no doubt unconsciously, an ultra-papalism reminiscent of the ultra-bolshevism ascribed by Merleau-Ponty to Sartre.[4] One further deduction, and Laínez would have turned the papacy into an institution warranted rather by the historical juncture

---

[1] Alberigo, *op. cit.* pp. 36 ff., 67 ff. The texts of Laínez are in H. Grisar (ed.), *Jacobi Lainez disputationes tridentinae* (2 vols., Vienna, 1886), I, 1–390; see esp. p. 175.

[2] Alberigo, *op. cit.* p. 83; cf. the Tridentine discussion on the ministry of confirmation, in his *I vescovi italiani al Concilio di Trento* (Florence, ? 1959), pp. 448 f.

[3] *Lo sviluppo della dottrina*, p. 84, n. 125.

[4] M. Merleau-Ponty, *Les aventures de la dialectique* (Paris, 1955), pp. 131 ff.

than by the word of God. Pius IV seems to have detected something of the kind, and Laínez went down with the curialist fathers little better than with the episcopalists.[1] One is left again feeling that the relation between the Jesuits and the papacy was a less simple matter than has often been made out.

It seems clear that Laínez had in mind the field of missionary activity. He had a particular sense of the importance of extra-European missions, and strongly encouraged Jesuits to pursue this vocation even at the expense of the European obligations of the society;[2] this explains why he showed less interest in England than Ignatius had.[3] But Englishmen ought not to need reminding that the word mission had and has no specially extra-European sense, implying rather a state of mind than a territorial region;[4] it is indeed surely significant that the Jesuits should have thought so much in terms of people and activity and so little in terms of territory. What Laínez was proposing at Trent, and what, morally speaking, it was unimaginable for the assembled bishops to have conceded, was that the Church, in its old ground as outside it, should put itself in an 'état de mission'.

Evennett points out that the practical outcome of this conflict was a compromise; the papacy could scarcely assent to the more extreme position of either side.[5] But since the compromise was in fact partially embodied in some sort of territorial division, the combination was a somewhat unstable mixture rather than a compound of its elements. Where the traditional structure of the Church remained in place, the century after Trent brought results which, like the reform decrees of the council, conformed more closely to the views of the episcopalist fathers than to those of Laínez. The Tridentine ideal of episcopal reform gained

---

[1] *Lo sviluppo della dottrina*, pp. 76 f., 95 f.

[2] Guibert, *La spiritualité de la Compagnie de Jésus*, p. 196; the connection was suggested at the council: Alberigo, *op. cit.* p. 85. Cf. Laínez, *Disputationes tridentinae*, p. 214.

[3] J. Crehan, 'St Ignatius and Cardinal Pole', *Archivum historicum Societatis Jesu*, XXV (1956), 96; Dickens, *English Reformation*, p. 280 and n. 57.

[4] Guibert, *op. cit.* p. 138 f., where he notes that Laínez would have considered himself *en mission* at Trent. Alberigo's remark (*op. cit.* pp. 104 f.) that the council was concerned with the problems of particular churches rather than with those of the universal Church is surely important.

[5] See above, pp. 99 f.

credit from finding immediate and thorough-going illustration in the work of Carlo Borromeo in Milan, 'the acknowledged model bishop', as Evennett says elsewhere, 'for the whole Catholic world, zealous, efficient, ascetic, tireless, charitable, selfless, uncompromising'.[1] The thesis that the Italian Counter-Reformation was simply an aristocratic reaction permitted by the collapse of the bases of the medieval Italian economy is neither fresh nor satisfying. But it might have been predicted that this refurbishing of hierarchical ideas and procedures, framed to impose on Italians, and not least on their sexual relations,[2] a rigid social and moral straitjacket, would in the long run and in less dedicated hands achieve a general stagnation. A recent discussion of Borromeo's nephew and successor Federico has described this development in language remarkable both for its precision and because it comes from a source where prejudice will hardly be suspected. 'One is struck'—in reading Borromeo's published collection of addresses to his diocesan synods, the *Sacri Ragionamenti*—'by the fact that these are directed not so much to an evangelisation of society...as to the conservation or re-establishment of a pre-existing order, and fall into a category which may clearly be described as *controriformistica*, not because they are a reaction to the infiltration of heresy...but because of the *preoccupazione restauratrice* which in them prevails over an interest in the problems of the time'.[3] One is struck indeed: Borromeo's chief objection to scandalous behaviour by his clergy seems to be that it will make a very poor show at the Last Judgment.[4]

[1] Hurstfield (ed.), *The Reformation crisis*, p. 70; cf. Jedin-Broutin, *L'évêque dans la tradition pastorale du xvi^e siècle*, pp. 97–107. There is a useful account of Borromeo's background in L. Cristiani, *L'Eglise à l'époque du Concile de Trente* (A. Fliche and V. Martin, *Histoire de l'Eglise*, XVII, *s.l.*, 1948), pp. 177–80.

[2] E. Cattaneo, 'Influenze veronese nella legislazione di San Carlo', in *Problemi di vita religiosa in Italia nel Cinquecento* (Padua, 1960), p. 139, for Borromeo's separation of men and women, first at communion, then in the body of the Duomo, then into separate churches. The author finds this an ideal 'molto positivo'.

[3] P. Prodi, Nel IV centinaio della nascita di Federico Borromeo: note biografiche e bibliografiche', *Convivium* (Bologna), XXXIII (1965), 337–59; passage quoted at p. 349.

[4] *I sacri ragionamenti sinodali di Federico Borromeo cardinale...ed arcivescovo di Milano* (10 vols.(!), Milan, 1632), II, 18:—'Si come nell'ordine generale del Mondo, mentre celebrerassi l'universal giudicio, grandissima sarà la turbazione

## The Spirit of the Counter-Reformation

Outside Italy, the Borromean ideal proved most readily acceptable in France: M. Orcibal has established for the reform programme of the French Church in the early seventeenth century a pedigree in which its immediate forebears are Carlo Borromeo and the Council of Trent.[1] Orcibal, attempting to clear up confusion engendered by indiscriminate use of the term Jansenist, has with other scholars pointed to the dominant role played in this revival by Pierre de Bérulle; and Bérulle's contribution to the Counter-Reformation seems to have been to take the hierarchical reformism of Trent and Borromeo and endow it with a now obligatory corresponding spirituality. After an upbringing in which the chief influences were Jesuit and mystical, Bérulle in 1602 underwent the Spiritual Exercises in what one cannot help feeling is rather aptly known as the *retraite de Verdun*. The upshot of this was that he decided not to enter the Society, and began to elaborate a spiritual doctrine, derived from the Christian neoplatonists, of which the notion of hierarchy was a central principle. This was a version of the idea of a Great Chain of Being: aiming at a 'compréhension surnaturelle de toute chose', Bérulle grasped the Church as, mediately through Christ, a divine emanation in which light and power descended through a hierarchy of orders identified in particular with the episcopate and the priesthood. In this system the proper attitude of the human creature was reverence, servitude, adoration; imitating the archetypal submission of Christ, the soul found its own level and let itself, as it were, float to the 'order' in which God had ordained it to be set.[2] The extent to which this hierarchy of stable states paralleled, assumed, and indeed incorporated the social and political hierarchies of seventeenth-century France

delle cose, perchè niuna di esse si ritroverà nel suo proprio luogo, ed in buono stato, essendo il tutto sottosopra rivolto...'

[1] J. Orcibal, *Le premier Port-Royal: Réforme ou Contre-réforme?* (Paris, Centre de Documentation Universitaire, 1956), and *Les origines du Jansénisme*, III (Louvain/ Paris, 1947), 25; Jedin-Broutin, *L'évêque dans la tradition pastorale du xviᵉ siècle*, pp. 104 f.—apparently by Broutin.

[2] P. Cochois, *Bérulle et l'école française* (Collection *Maîtres Spirituels*, Paris, 1963), pp. 25–33, 124–33 (the *Editions du Seuil* deserve great credit for this admirable series of little books); also J. Dagens, *Bérulle et les origines de la restauration catholique, 1571–1611* (s.l., 1952), pp. 181 ff., and L. Cognet, *Les origines de la spiritualité française au xviiᵉ siècle* (Paris, 1949), p. 9.

has been noticed by several commentators, and is fairly explicit in Bérulle himself.[1] Orcibal makes it clear that Saint-Cyran, no doubt the most controversial figure of the seventeenth-century Church, was above all a faithful continuator of Bérulle, and that his doctrine stands squarely in the Tridentine and Borromean tradition. As for other expressions of it, Borromeo provided a clear and conscious precedent for the teaching of Arnauld's *Frequent Communion*. Identical recommendations about the reception of communion may have acquired a somewhat original flavour when filtered through Bérulle's psychology of reverence; but there seems no reason to disagree with Orcibal's view that the book belongs 'non pas dans le prétendu bloc janséniste, mais parmi les manifestations les plus élevées de la Contre-réforme'.[2] Whether it was not rather too elevated for Englishmen or Paraguayan Indians is another question.

For if Bérulle, Saint-Cyran and Arnauld are taken as authentic representatives of the hierarchical mode which post-Reformation Catholicism predominantly followed in regions of religious continuity, some difficulties which arose in the Catholicism of other parts of Europe, and outside it, emerge as more intelligible than they have often seemed. One may find them, of course, in China; but there is no need to go so far afield. In France, as in the Netherlands, areas of successful ecclesiastical restoration abutted on areas where society had been or was going through the mangle of Reformation, and Catholicism was called to undergo transformations for which only a missionary notion of the Church could properly provide. The Catholicisms of England and the northern Netherlands had been labouring with this problem since the end of the sixteenth century, in England generally to the advantage of the missionaries, who had to their credit the heroisms and achievements of the Elizabethan period, in Holland to the advantage of the hierarchicals, whom the ecclesiastical reconstruction of 1559 enabled to practise a sort of suspended Tridentinism. Something of what these controversies implied

[1] Cochois, *op. cit.* p. 31.
[2] Orcibal, *Le premier Port-Royal*, p. 26; also his *Saint-Cyran et le Jansénisme* (Collection *Maîtres Spirituels*, Paris, 1961), pp. 39 f.

*The Spirit of the Counter-Reformation*

may be seen in the charge of moral laxity which the Dutch vicar apostolic, Sasbout Vosmeer, brought against the Dutch Jesuits for permitting their penitents to attend the University of Leiden and invest in the East India Company.[1] The Bérullian model had a disastrous effect on the Catholicism of these regions. In Holland it produced after three quarters of a century the neat solution of a schismatic Church consisting mainly of bishops and a flock entirely without them.[2] The existence in England of a Catholicism which without visible decay survived the lack of bishops for fifty years had always been felt rather disturbing in France; in 1624 Bérulle and Richelieu collaborated in an ecclesiastical-political operation partly intended to impose on English Catholics as bishop the very unsuitable Richard Smith, qualified chiefly by long-standing familiarity with Richelieu and ideological alliance with Bérulle.[3] It was immediately obvious that the hierarchical approach was ludicrously inadaptable to English conditions; any sympathy it might arouse would come not from Catholics but from Laudian Anglicans.[4] In England the chief consequence of this attempt was to ensure that Catholics were left for another half-century without leadership and without guidance as to their correct status in the Church. It had more immediate repercussions in France itself, where Saint-Cyran seized the opportunity, in pouncing on the English Jesuits, to make drastically clear his view of the incompatibility of hierarchical

[1] L. J. Rogier, *Geschiedenis van het Katholicisme in Noord-Nederland in de 16ᵉ en de 17ᵉ Eeuw*, II (Amsterdam, 1946), 60. There is a summary of this notable work in A. G. Weiler, O. J. de Jong, L. J. Rogier and C. W. Mönnick, *Geschiedenis van de Kerk in Nederland* (Utrecht/Antwerp, 1962), pp. 167–233, 'De katholieke kerk van 1559 tot 1795'; cf. p. 192 for the point here.

[2] Rogier, in *Geschiedenis van de Kerk in Nederland*, pp. 205–25; on the general question of missionary and hierarchical conceptions in the northern Netherlands, Rogier has important remarks in *Geschiedenis van het Katholicisme*, II, 77 f., especially 79: 'The foundation of Propaganda was a kind of papal recognition of the fact that world-hegemony had passed to the Republic [of the Netherlands] and England.'

[3] A. F. Allison, 'Richard Smith, Richelieu and the French marriage', *Recusant History*, VII (1964), 148–211, especially 148 f., 164 f., 185 f.; Cochois, *Bérulle et l'école française*, pp. 44 f., and Orcibal, below. For a later stage of the problem in England, T. A. Birrell, 'English Catholics without a bishop, 1655–1672', *Recusant History*, IV (1958), 142–78.

[4] Stephen Gough, Laud's chaplain, became a Catholic and entered the Oratory in 1645: G. Albion, *Charles I and the court of Rome* (Louvain, 1935), p. 197.

and missionary conceptions of the Church,[1] and so set in train the crisis of the French Counter-Reformation.

*Petrus Aurelius* gave a straight answer to Laínez's Tridentine theses. It was natural that the problem should have become most clearly visible along the European frontier between traditional and missionary Catholicism; and it seems equally significant that Saint-Cyran should have taken what might appear to be a trivial dispute about the respective rights of bishops and religious orders, and have constructed it as a fundamental conflict between a rigidly conceived divine ordinance and the powers of human effort and invention.[2]

Conflicts of this nature were surely inevitable, and do not in themselves explain the petering out of the Counter-Reformation. The papacy claimed and wielded overriding power in order to resolve precisely such problems; it must in the end be held responsible for the fact that, in a region and a period decisive for the reshaping of European society, these were allowed to culminate in almost total deadlock. In his two final lectures Evennett spoke of the modifications of the counter-reformation papacy as a necessary and constructive response to the changed conception of a properly Christian life which he had earlier described. If he were to have reconsidered them today, I doubt if he would have changed their essential outline; but in the light of two lines of recent investigation I think he would have conceded that in some very important respects the conversion was a modernisation *manquée*.

The great achievement of M. Delumeau's large study of late sixteenth-century Rome[3] has been to present for its period an economic, not merely a financial, history of the papacy. He starts from the accepted view[4] that the chief characteristic of the

---

[1] In the works published under the name Petrus Aurelius: *Petri Aurelii theologi opera, iussu et impensis cleri gallicani denuo in lucem edita* (3 vols., Paris, 1646); cf. Orcibal, *Saint-Cyran et le Jansénisme*, pp. 15 f.; on relations between Saint-Cyran, Smith and the Dutch vicar apostolic Rovenius, also Rogier, *Geschiedenis van het Katholicisme*, ii, 118, and Philip Hughes, *Rome and the Counter-Reformation in England* (London, 1942), p. 360.          [2] Orcibal, *op. cit.* p. 17.
[3] J. Delumeau, *Vie sociale et économique de Rome dans la seconde moitié du xvi^e siècle* (2 vols., continuous pagination, Paris, 1957–9).          [4] See above, p. 94.

economics of the post-Reformation papacy was the shift from a base in Christendom at large to one limited to the papal state; he shows in detail how the financial techniques used to exploit its resources were not only, as in the development of taxation and the sale of public office, comparable to those of the most sophisticated secular governments, but in one important field, in the foundation of a secure and attractive system of public credit, far in advance of them. It is clear that much of the buoyancy of the late sixteenth-century papacy was due to its success in channelling the savings of Italy into its coffers.[1] Delumeau describes, on the other hand, the breakdown and abandonment of the corresponding effort made by some contemporary Popes, especially by Sixtus V, to encourage the economic development of Rome and the papal state. Despite a number of conditions favourable in particular to the development of a textile industry —capital, labour, a large market, sheep, alum—Rome after 1600 became a city whose only industries, building above all, were unproductive ones, and where the very success of the Popes in public finance, unbalanced by industrial development, produced a society of *rentiers*; while the population of the backward state was overtaxed to pay for the universal enterprises of the Church.[2] The general picture of economic decay in the Mediterranean world emerges from Delumeau's work confirmed by the growing imbalance of the papal budget after 1600 as the cost of servicing debt rose to equal the annual revenue, and the collapse about 1620 of the market for papal alum in northern Europe, constant, despite all other difficulties, until then.[3] It may be that Delumeau's thoughts about the opening at this point of a 'fossé...entre l'Eglise et le monde du travail'[4] reflect a little too immediately the problems of the French Church in the 1950s; but there is surely something in his point that the artistic production of seventeenth-century Rome reflects, in its quantity and in its subject-matter, some divorce of this kind. If the general pattern of the Counter-Reformation here suggested is correct, his picture

[1] Delumeau, *op. cit.* pp. 783 f.          [2] *Ibid.* pp. 501–17, 824 f.
[3] *Ibid.* pp. 744 f., 822 f.; and his *L'alun de Rome, xvᵉ–xixᵉ siècle*, (Paris, 1962) pp. 45–8, 207, 214 f.
[4] *Vie sociale et économique de Rome*, p. 516.

of a Roman art 'luxueux comme elle (Rome), mais oublieux, comme elle, de la valeur divine et humaine du travail'[1] will have its relevance to the decay of Catholicism in the seventeenth century.

There is much similarity between Delumeau's conclusions and those which seem to be emerging from a large-scale German enterprise designed to analyse the governmental structure of the papacy in this period. The first volume of a projected series has described in exhaustive detail how the formal modernisation of papal government in the late sixteenth century was something of an aspiration, which only achieved reality after a long period of conflict between bureaucratic and patrimonial attitudes, illustrated for the pontificate in question by the efforts of the secretariat of state to maintain itself against the enveloping influence of the cardinal nephew Barberini.[2] It is at present not easy to get this conflict into proper perspective; but it seems likely to have been responsible for a good deal of the incompetence shown by the papacy in its handling of north-European problems during this crucial period. One of the earliest jobs to be thrown to Barberini was the protectorship of England;[3] George Con, the nuncio sent to England in 1636, was his servant and seems, in his mixture of superficial culture, snobbery and ambition, to have been a horse fairly typical of the stable.[4] Apart from inaugurating the fifty years during which Rome evaded a decision on the status of the English mission, Barberini's administration may be remembered for suppressing out of hand what was perhaps the most remarkable inspiration of English missionary Catholicism, Mary Ward's Institute of Mary. In the long list of motives for this act, Tridentine rigour and sexual vulgarity are strongly and about equally represented; it makes a sadly comprehensive anthology of the reasons for not being a Catholic in the seventeenth century.[5] The papacy, if I may quote Kraus's

---

[1] *Ibid.* p. 517.

[2] A. Kraus, *Das päpstliche Staatssekretariat unter Urban VIII, 1623–1644* (Forschungen zur Geschichte des päpstlichen Staatssekretariats, Bd. I, Rome, etc., 1964), especially pp. 270–5.    [3] *Ibid.* p. 12.

[4] *Ibid.* pp. 144 f.; Albion, *Charles I and the court of Rome*, chs. 5–12.

[5] P. Guilday, *The English Catholic refugees on the continent* (London, 1914), pp. 163–208; also above, p. 85 and n.

conclusion in a somewhat wider context than that intended, 'did not break in the tension between its task and its nature, but that it produced no constructive statesman in a time of exceptional changes was a disastrous handicap for the time to come'[1]. By the death of Urban VIII in 1644, the moment would seem to have passed when Catholicism could have established itself at any depth in the heart of the rising civilisation of northern Europe. A hundred and fifty years of crippling immobility were to ensue before, ironically, the progress of industrial change presented the papacy with a windfall which it had not entirely deserved, and showed little imagination in exploiting.

*Belfast, 1966*

[1] Kraus, *op. cit.* p. 275.

# LIST OF WORKS CITED

Albareda, A. *Sant Ignasi a Montserrat.* Monestir de Montserrat, 1935.
'Intorno alla scuola di orazione metodica stabilita a Monserrato dall'Abate Garsias Jimenez de Cisneros', *Archivum historicum Societatis Jesu,* XXV (1956), 254 ff.
Alberigo, G. *I vescovi italiani al Concilio di Trento.* Florence, ?1959.
'Diplomazia e vita della Chiesa nel XVI secolo', *Critica storica* (Florence), I (1962), 49 ff.
*Lo sviluppo della dottrina sui poteri nella Chiesa universale.* Rome/Freiburg-im-B., 1964.
'The Council of Trent: new views on the occasion of its 4th centenary', *Concilium,* VII, no. 1 (September, 1965), 38 ff.
Albion, G. *Charles I and the court of Rome.* Louvain, 1935.
Allison, A. F. 'Richard Smith, Richelieu and the French marriage', *Recusant History,* VII (1964), 148 ff.
Altamira y Crevea, R. *Historia de España y de la civilización española.* Various editions, Barcelona, 1900– .
Asín Palacios, M. *La escatología musulmana en la Divina Comedia.* Madrid, 1919.
Aubenas, R. and Ricard, R. *See* Fliche.
Aurelius, Petrus. *See* Duvergier de Hauranne.
Austrian Cultural Institute in Rome, etc. *Nuntiaturberichte aus Deutschland.* Vienna etc., 1897– : in progress.
Bataillon, M. 'Sur la diffusion des oeuvres de Savonarole en Espagne et en Portugal, 1500–1560', in *Mélanges...offerts à M. Joseph Vianey* (Paris, 1934), pp. 93 ff.
'De Savonarole à Louis de Grenade', *Revue de littérature comparée,* XVI (1936), 23ff.
*Erasme et l'Espagne.* Paris, 1937.
Battersby, W. J. *De la Salle: a pioneer of modern education.* London, 1949.
*De la Salle: saint and spiritual writer.* London, 1950.
(ed.) *De la Salle: letters and documents.* London, 1952.
Baur, F. C. *Die Epochen der kirchlichen Geschichtsschreibung.* Tübingen, 1852.
Beltrán de Heredia, V. *Historia de la reforma de la Provincia [O.P.] de España.* ?Madrid, 1939.
*Las corrientes de espiritualidad entre los Domínicos de Castilla durante la primera mitad del siglo XVI.* Salamanca, 1941.
Bianconi, A. *L'opera delle Compagnie del Divino Amore nella riforma cattolica.* Città di Castello, 1914.
Binns, L. Elliott *The history of the decline and fall of the mediaeval papacy.* London, 1934.
Birrell, T. A. 'English Catholics without a bishop, 1655–72', *Recusant History,* IV (1958), 142 ff.

# List of Works Cited

Blet, P. *Le clergé de France et la monarchie: étude sur les Assemblées Générales du Clergé de 1615 à 1666.* 2 vols., Rome, 1959.

Boehmer, H. *Loyola und die deutsche Mystik.* Sächsischen Akademie der Wissenschaften, phil.-hist. Klasse, Bd. XXIII, Heft 1, Leipzig, 1921.

Borromeo, F. *Sacri ragionamenti sinodali.* 10 vols., Milan, 1632.

Bossy, John 'Rome and the Elizabethan Catholics: a question of geography', *The Historical Journal,* VII (1964), 137 ff.
— 'The character of Elizabethan Catholicism', in T. Aston (ed.), *Crisis in Europe, 1560–1660* (London, 1965), pp. 223 ff.

Braudel, F. *La Méditerranée et le monde méditerranéen à l'époque de Philippe II.* Paris, 1949.

Bremond, H. *Histoire littéraire du sentiment religieux en France depuis la fin des guerres de religion jusqu'à nos jours.* 12 vols., Paris, 1916–36.
— *A literary history of religious thought in France.* English translation of first 3 vols. of above, London, 1928–36.

Broutin, P. *See* Jedin, H.

*Catholic Encyclopedia. See* Herbermann.

Cattaneo, E. 'Influenze veronese nella legislazione di San Carlo [Borromeo]' in *Problemi di vita religiosa in Italia nel Cinquecento* (Padua, 1960), pp. 123 ff.

Célier, L. 'Alexandre VI et la réforme de l'Eglise', *Mélanges d'archéologie et d'histoire* (Ecole française de Rome), XXVII (1907), 65 ff.
— *Les dataires du XVe siècle et les origines de la Daterie Apostolique.* Paris, 1910.

Chadwick, O. *The Reformation.* Pelican History of the Church, III, Harmondsworth, 1964.

Cistellini, A. *Figure della riforma pretridentina.* Brescia, 1948.

Cochois, P. *Bérulle et l'école française [de spiritualité].* Collection *Maîtres Spirituels,* Paris, 1963.

Cognet, L. *Les origines de la spiritualité française au XVIIe siècle.* Paris, 1949.
— *De la dévotion moderne à la spiritualité française.* Paris, 1958.
— *Post-Reformation spirituality.* English translation of above, London, 1959.

Colombás, G. M. *Un reformador benedictino en tiempo de los Reyes Católicos: García Jimenez de Cisneros, abad de Montserrat.* Montserrat, 1955.

*Concilium Tridentinum. See* Görresgesellschaft.

Coulton, G. G. *Five centuries of religion.* 4 vols., Cambridge, 1923–50.

Crehan, J. 'St Ignatius and Cardinal Pole', *Archivum historicum Societatis Jesu,* XXV (1956), 72 ff.

Crisógono de Jesús Sacramentado *San Juan de la Cruz.* 2 vols., Madrid, 1929.

Cristiani, L. *See* Fliche.

Dagens, J. *Bérulle et les origines de la restauration catholique, 1571–1611.* S.l., 1952.

Delaruelle, E., Labande, E.-R. and Ourliac, P. *See* Fliche.

Delumeau, J. *Vie économique et sociale de Rome pendant la deuxième moitié du XVIe siècle.* 2 vols., Rome, 1957–9.
— *L'alun de Rome, XVe–XIXe siècle.* Paris, 1962.

# List of Works Cited

Denifle, H. S. *Luther und Luthertum in der ersten Entwicklung*. 2 vols., Mainz, 1903–9. *Ergänzungen*, 2 vols., Mainz, 1905–6.

Dickens, A. G. *The English Reformation*. London, 1964.

*Dictionnaire de spiritualité*. See Viller.

*Dictionnaire de théologie catholique*. See Vacant.

Dittrich, F. 'Beiträge zur Geschichte der katholischen Reformation im ersten Drittel des 16. Jahrhunderts', *Historisches Jahrbuch* (Görresgesellschaft), v (1884), 319 ff.; vii (1886), 1 ff.

*Gasparo Contarini, 1483–1542*. Braunsberg, 1885.

Döllinger, J. J. I. von *Beiträge zur politischen, kirchlichen und Cultur-Geschichte der sechs letzten Jahrhunderte*. 3 vols., Regensburg/Vienna, 1862–82.

Dudon, P. *Saint Ignace de Loyola*. Paris, 1934.

Dupront, A. 'Du Concile de Trente: réflexions autour d'un IVe centenaire', *Revue historique*, ccvi (1951), 262 ff.

'Le Concile de Trente', in B. Botte and others, *Le Concile et les conciles* (*s.l.*, 1960), 202 ff.

*Les conciles de l'Eglise moderne et contemporaine*, i. Centre de Documentation Universitaire, Paris, 1963.

Duvergier de Hauranne, Jean, abbé de Saint-Cyran *Petri Aurelii theologi opera*. 3 vols., Paris, 1646.

Elkan, A. 'Entstehung und Entwicklung des Begriffes Gegenreformation', *Historische Zeitschrift*, cxii (1924), 473 ff.

Elton, G. R. *Reformation Europe, 1517–59*. London, 1963.

*Enciclopedia cattolica*. See Paschini.

Evennett, H. O. *The Counter-Reformation*. Catholic Truth Society, London, 1935.

'The New Orders', in G. R. Elton (ed.), *The New Cambridge Modern History: II, The Reformation* (Cambridge, 1958), ch. ix.

'The Counter-Reformation', in J. Hurstfield (ed.), *The Reformation crisis* (London, 1965), 58 ff.

Farrell, A. P. *The Jesuit code of liberal education*. Milwaukee, 1938.

Febvre, L. *Pour une histoire à part entière*. Paris, 1962.

Feine, H. E. *Kirchliche Rechtsgeschichte, Bd. I: Die katholische Kirche*. 2nd ed., Weimar, 1954.

Fitzpatrick, E. A. *St Ignatius and the Ratio Studiorum*. New York, 1933.

Fliche, A., Martin, V. and others (eds.). *Histoire de l'Eglise depuis les origines jusqu'à nos jours*. *S.l.*, 1934– : in progress.

    xiv, part ii: Delaruelle, E., Labande, E.-R., Ourliac, P. *L'Eglise au temps du Grand Schisme et de la crise conciliaire*, ii. 1964.

    xv: Aubenas, R. and Ricard, R. *L'Eglise et la Renaissance, 1449–1517*. 1951.

    xvii: Cristiani, L. *L'Eglise a l'époque du Concile de Trente*. 1948.

Ganss, G. E. *St Ignatius' idea of a Jesuit university*. Milwaukee, 1954; 2nd ed., 1956.

García Villoslada, R. 'San Ignacio de Loyola y Erasmo de Rotterdam', *Estudios eclesiásticos*, xvi (1942), 244 ff.

German Historical Institute in Rome. *Nuntiaturberichte aus Deutschland*. Gotha, etc., 1892– : in progress.

# List of Works Cited

Gilmont, J.-F. and Daman, P. *Bibliographie ignatienne.* Louvain, 1958.

Giuliani, M. and others. *Finding God in all things: essays in Jesuit spirituality selected from* Christus. English translation by Wm. J. Young, Chicago, 1958.

Görresgesellschaft. *Concilium Tridentinum: diariorum, epistularum, tractatuum nova collectio.* Freiburg-im-B., 1901– : in progress.

Gothein, E. *Ignatius von Loyola und die Gegenreformation.* Halle, 1895.

Graham, Aelred 'The pathos of Vatican II', *Encounter* (December 1965).

Grisar, H. (ed.) *Jacobi Lainez disputationes tridentinae.* 2 vols., Vienna, 1886.

Grisar, J. *Die ersten Anklagen in Rom gegen das Institut Maria Wards.* Rome, 1959.

Groult, P. *Les mystiques des Pays-Bas et la littérature espagnole du seizième siècle.* Louvain, 1927.

Guibert, J. de 'Le généralat de Claude Aquaviva (1581–1615): sa place dans l'histoire de la spiritualité de la Compagnie de Jésus', *Archivum historicum Societatis Jesu,* X (1941), 59 ff.

*La spiritualité de la Compagnie de Jésus.* Rome, 1953.

Guilday, P. *The English Catholic refugees on the continent.* London, 1914.

Guillermou, A. *Saint Ignace de Loyola et la Compagnie de Jésus.* Collection *Maîtres Spirituels,* Paris, 1960.

Hefele, C. J. von *Der Cardinal Ximenes und die kirchlichen Zustände Spaniens am Ende des 15. und Anfange des 16. Jahrhunderts.* Tübingen, 1844.

*The Life of Cardinal Ximenes.* English translation of above, London, 1860.

Heimbucher, M. *Die Orden und Kongregationen der katholischen Kirche.* 2 vols., Paderborn, 1933–4.

Herbermann, C. G. and others (eds.). *The Catholic Encyclopedia.* 16 vols., New York, 1907–14.

Herre, P. *Papsttum und Papstwahl im Zeitalter Philipps II.* Leipzig, 1907.

Hicks, L. 'Mary Ward's great enterprise', *The Month,* CLI–CLIII (1928–9).

(ed.) *Letters and memorials of Robert Persons: I, to 1588.* Catholic Record Society, XXXIX, London, 1942.

Höfler, C. A. C. von *Die romanische Welt und ihr Verhältnis zu den Reformideen des Mittelalters.* Sitzungsberichte der Wiener Akademie, phil.-hist. Klasse, XCI, 1878.

Hofmann, W. von *Forschungen zur Geschichte der kurialen Behörden vom Schisma bis zur Reformation.* 2 vols., Rome, 1914.

Hughes, Philip. *Rome and the Counter-Reformation in England.* London, 1942.

Hyma, A. *The Christian Renaissance: a history of the Devotio Moderna.* New York, 1925.

Ignatius of Loyola, St. *Obras completas de S. Ignacio de Loyola.* Ed. V. Larrañaga, *Biblioteca de autores cristianos,* LXXXVI, Madrid, 1952.

*Spiritual Exercises. See* Longridge; Monumenta Historica Societatis Jesu.

Iparraguirre, I. *Historia de la práctica de los Ejercicios espirituales de San Ignacio: I, Práctica de los Ejercicios...en vida de su autor, 1522–56.* Bilbao/Rome, 1946.

*Introduzione allo studio degli Esercizi Spirituali di San Ignacio.* Rome, 1951.

*Orientaciones bibliográficas sobre S. Ignacio de Loyola.* Rome, 1957.

*See* Monumenta Historica Societatis Jesu; Leturia.

# List of Works Cited

Janssen, J. *Geschichte des deutschen Volkes seit dem Ausgang des Mittelalters.* Various eds., Freiburg-im-B., 1878–1917.
　*History of the German people at (after) the close of the Middle Ages.* English translation of above, 17 vols., London, 1896–1925.
Jedin, H. *Girolamo Seripando: sein Leben und Denken im Geisteskampf des 16. Jahrhunderts.* 2 vols., Würzburg, 1937.
　*Papal legate at the Council of Trent: Cardinal Seripando.* English translation of vol. I of above, St Louis/London, 1947.
　*Katholische Reformation oder Gegenreformation? Ein Versuch zur Klärung der Begriffe.* Luzern, 1946.
　*Il tipo ideale di vescovo secondo la riforma cattolica.* Brescia, 1950.
　and Broutin, P. *L'evêque dans la tradition pastorale du XVIe siècle.* French translation of above, with additions, Bruges, 1953.
　'Ein "Turmerlebnis" des jungen Contarini', *Historisches Jahrbuch*, LXX (1951), 115 ff.
　*Geschichte des Konzils von Trient.* Freiburg-im-B., 1949– : in progress.
　*History of the Council of Trent.* English translation of above, 2 vols. to date, London, 1957–61.
　*Tommaso Campeggio (1483–1564): tridentinische Reform und kuriale Tradition.* Münster, 1958.
　*Ecumenical councils of the Catholic Church.* English translation of *Kleine Konziliengeschichte*, Freiburg-im-B., etc., 1960.
Just, L. 'Neue Arbeiten zur Geschichte des Konzils von Trient', *Archivfür Reformationsgeschichte*, XLIV (1953), 240 ff.
Kerker, J. 'Die kirchliche Reform in Italien unmittelbar vor dem Tridentinum', *Tübinger theologische Quartalschrift*, XLI (1859), 3 ff.
Kidd, B. J. *The Counter-Reformation.* London, 1933.
Knowles, David *The religious orders in England.* 3 vols., Cambridge, 1950–9.
Kraus, A. *Das päpstliche Staatssekretariat unter Urban VIII, 1623–1644. Forschungen zur Geschichte des päpstlichen Staatssekretariats*, Bd. I, Rome etc., 1964.
Laínez, Diego. *See* Grisar, H.
Larrañaga, V. *La espiritualidad de S. Ignacio comparada con la de S. Teresa de Jesús.* Madrid, 1944. *See* Ignatius.
Le Bras, G. *Introduction à l'histoire de la pratique religieuse en France.* 2 vols., Paris, 1942–5.
Leturia, P. 'Pastor, España y la restauración católica', *Razon y Fe*, LXXXV (1928), 136 ff.
　'Génesis de los ejercicios de San Ignacio y su influjo en la fundación de la Compañía de Jesús (1521–40)', *Archivum historicum Societatis Jesus*, x (1941), 16 ff.
　'¿Hizo San Ignacio en Montserrat o en Manresa vida solitaria?', in *Estudios ignacianos*, I, 113 ff.
　ed. and revised by I. Iparraguirre *Estudios ignacianos*. 2 vols., Rome, 1957.
Longridge, W. H. (ed.) *The Spiritual Exercises of Saint Ignatius of Loyola, translated from the Spanish with a commentary and a translation of the Directorium in Exercitia.* London, 1919; Everyman's Library, 1930.

# List of Works Cited

Macaulay, T. B. 'Ranke's *History of the Popes*', in *Critical and historical essays* (Everyman's Library, 2 vols., London/New York, 1907), II, 38 ff.

Martz, Louis, L. *The poetry of meditation*. Yale Studies in English, CXXV, New Haven/London, 1954.

Maurenbrecher, W. *Geschichte der katholischen Reformation*. Vol. I only published, Nordlingen, 1880.

Merleau-Ponty, M. *Les aventures de la dialectique*. Paris, 1955.

Mestwerdt, P. *Die Anfänge des Erasmus: Humanismus und Devotio Moderna*. Leipzig, 1917.

Monica, Sister. *Angela Merici and her teaching idea*. London, 1927.

Monumenta Historica Societatis Jesu:
*Exercitia spiritualia Sancti Ignatii de Loyola et eorum directoria*. Monumenta Ignatiana, series II, Madrid, 1919.

*Directoria exercitiorum spiritualium, 1540–99*. Ed. I. Iparraguirre, Monument Ignatiana, series II, nova editio, vol. II, Rome, 1955.

*Constitutiones*. Monumenta Ignatiana, series III, vol. III, Rome, 1938.

Müller, A. V. *Luthers theologische Quellen: seine Verteidigung gegen Denifle und Grisar*. Giessen, 1912.

Muller, H. (?pseud.) *Les origines de la Compagnie de Jésus: Ignace et Lainez*. Paris, 1898.

Nicolau, M. *Jerónimo Nadal (1507–80), sus obras y doctrinas espirituales*. Madrid, 1949.

*Nuntiaturberichte aus Deutschland*. See Austrian Cultural, German Historical Institute in Rome.

Nuttall, G. F. *Richard Baxter*. London, 1965.

Orcibal, J. *Les origines du Jansénisme*. Louvain/Paris, 1947– : in progress.

*Le premier Port-Royal: Réforme ou Contre-Réforme?* Centre de Documentation Universitaire, Paris, 1956.

*Saint-Cyran et le Jansénisme*. Collection *Maîtres Spirituels*, Paris, 1961.

Parsons, Robert *The first booke of the Christian exercise, appertayning to resolution*. [Rouen,] 1582.

Paschini, P. *La beneficenza in Italia e le Compagnie del Divino Amore nei primi decenni del Cinquecento*. Rome, 1925.

*Tre ricerche sulla storia della Chiesa nel Cinquecento*. Including reprint of above, Rome, 1945.

*S. Gaetana da Thiene, G. P. Carafa e le origini dei chierici regolari Teatini*. Rome, 1926.

and others (eds.). *Enciclopedia cattolica*. 12 vols., Vatican City, 1949–53.

Pastor, L. von *Geschichte der Päpste seit dem Ausgang des Mittelalters bis zum Tode Pius' VI*. Various editions, Freiburg-im-B., 1889– .

*The history of the Popes, from the close of the Middle Ages*. English translation of above, 40 vols., London, 1891–1953.

Peers, E. Allison *Studies of the Spanish mystics*. 3 vols., London, 1927–60.

*St John of the Cross and other lectures and addresses*. London, 1946.

Pescheck, C. A. *Geschichte der Gegenreformation in Böhmen*. 2 vols., Dresden/Leipzig, 1844.

Philippson, M. *Les origines du catholicisme moderne: la contre-révolution religieuse au XVIe siècle*. Brussels, 1884.

151

# List of Works Cited

Pinard de la Boullaye, H. *Saint Ignace de Loyola, directeur d'âmes*. Paris, 1947.

(ed.) *La spiritualité ignatienne: textes choisis et présentés par H.P.* Paris, 1949.

*Les étapes de rédaction des Exercices de S. Ignace*. Paris, 1950.

Plöchl, W. M. *Geschichte des Kirchenrechts*, vol. III, part I. Vienna/Munich, 1959.

Post, R. R. *De moderne devotie*. Amsterdam, 1940.

Premoli, O. M. *Fra Battista da Crema secondo documenti inediti*. Rome, 1910. *Storia dei Barnabiti*. 3 vols., Rome, 1913–25.

Prodi, P. 'Nel IV centinaio della nascita di Federico Borromeo: note biografiche e bibliografiche', *Convivium* (Bologna), XXXIII (1965), 337 ff.

Prussian Historical Institute in Rome. *See* German Historical Institute in Rome.

Rahner, Hugo *Ignatius von Loyola und das geschichtliche Werden seiner Frömmigkeit*. Vienna, 1947.

*The spirituality of St Ignatius Loyola*. English translation of above, Westminster, Md., 1953.

(ed.) *St Ignatius Loyola: letters to women*. Freiburg-im-B./Edinburgh, 1960.

Rahner, Karl *The dynamic element in the Church*. Freiburg-im-B./London, 1964.

Ranke, L. von *Fürsten und Völker von Süd-Europa im sechzehnten und siebzehnten Jahrhundert*. 4 vols., Berlin, 1836–8.

*The history of the Popes during the last four centuries*. English translation of vols. II–IV of above, 3 vols., London, 1908.

*Deutsche Geschichte im Zeitalter der Reformation*. 5 vols., Berlin, 1839–52.

Rigault, G. *Histoire générale de l'Institut des Frères des Ecoles Chrétiennes*. 9 vols., Paris, 1937–53.

Ritter, M. *Deutsche Geschichte im Zeitalter der Gegenreformation und des dreissigjährigen Krieges*. 3 vols., Stuttgart, 1889–1908.

Rogier, L. J. *Geschiedenis van het Katholicisme in Noord-Nederland in de 16e. en de 17e. Eeuw*. 3 vols., Amsterdam, 1945–6.

'De katholieke kerk van 1559 tot 1795', in A. G. Weiler and others, *Geschiedenis van de Kerk in Nederland* (Utrecht/Antwerp, 1962), pp. 167 ff.

Rupp, Gordon *Luther's progress to the Diet of Worms*. London, 1951. *The righteousness of God*. London, 1953.

Sanchís Alventosa, J. *La escuela mística alemana y sus relaciones con nuestros místicos del Siglo de Oro*. Madrid, 1946.

Schmitz, P. *Histoire de l'ordre de Saint Benoît*. 7 vols., Gembloux/Maredsous, 1942–56.

Tacchi-Venturi, P. *Storia della Compagnia di Gesù in Italia, I: La vita religiosa in Italia durante la prima età della Compagnia di Gesù*. 2nd ed., Rome, 1931.

Tierney, B. 'A conciliar theory of the thirteenth century', *Catholic Historical Review*, XXXVI (1951), 415 ff.

*Foundations of the conciliar theory*. Cambridge, 1955.

Trevor-Roper, H. R. 'Religion, the Reformation and social change', in G. A. Hayes-McCoy (ed.), *Historical studies, IV: papers read before the fifth Irish Conference of Historians* (London, 1963), pp. 18 ff.

# List of Works Cited

Vacant, A., Mangenot, E. and Amann, E. (eds.) *Dictionnaire de théologie catholique*. 15 vols., Paris, 1903–50.

Viller, M. and others (eds.). *Dictionnaire de spiritualité*. Paris, 1932– : in progress.

Watrigant, H. 'La genèse des Exercices de Saint Ignace de Loyola', *Etudes*, LXXI (1897), 506 ff.; LXXII, 195 ff.; LXXIII, 199 ff.

*La méditation fondamentale avant S. Ignace*. Enghien, 1907.

'La méditation méthodique et l'école des Frères de la Vie Commune', *Revue d'ascétique et de mystique*, III (1922), 134 ff.

'La méditation méthodique et Jean Mauburnus', *ibid.* IV (1923), 13 ff.

Weber, Max *The Protestant ethic and the spirit of capitalism*. English translation, London, 1930.

White, Helen C. *English devotional literature, 1600–1640*. Madison, Wisc., 1931.

# INDEX

For individual popes, offices of the papal curia, and religious orders
see under *popes, papal curia, religious orders.*

# Index

# Index

157

# Index

popes
  Adrian VI, 11
  Alexander VI, 111
  Calixtus III, 110
  Clement, VII, 106, 111
  Clement VIII, 122
  Eugenius IV, 110
  Gregory XIII, 8, 106, 107, 114, 116, 117, 122; and nunciatures, 118–21
  Gregory XV, and *Propaganda*, 122
  Innocent VIII, 104, 109, 116
  Julius II, 94, 100
  Julius III, 104, 106, 113
  Leo X, 100, 109, 112, 116
  Leo XIII, and Vatican Archives, 15
  Marcellus II, 112
  Martin V, 104, 116, 117
  Nicholas V, 110
  Paul III, 7, 28, 47, 106, 112, 113, 114, 116
  Paul IV, 10, 11, 106, 112, 113
  Paul V, 7
  Paul VI, 128 n.
  Pius II, 110
  Pius IV, 113–14, 137
  Pius V, 106, 114, 118, 120, 123
  Pius IX, 4
  Sixtus IV, and curia, 103, 105, 110
  Sixtus V, 8, 21, 94, 106, 107, 113, 118, 122–3; and congregations of cardinals, 114–16; economic policy of, 143
  Urban VIII, 144–5
priesthood, theory and practice of, 37, 39, 75–6, 83, 136

quietism, 19
Quinzani, Stefana, 27

Radewijns, Florent, 33
Rahner, Hugo, 126–7, 129–30
Rahner, Karl, 126–7, 130
Rancé, Armand de, 20
Ranke, L. von, 5–6, 10, 15, 16
religious orders: study of, 13, 68–9; Counter-Reformation and, 67–88 *passim*; pre-Reformation efforts at reform of old, 69–72; new, 73–88; and bishops, 99–100
religious orders, etc., of men:
  Alexian Brothers, 87
  Augustinian friars, 27, 69, 70
  *Barmherziger Brüder*, 87
  Barnabites, 17, 74

Benedictines, 27, 34–5, 58–9, 69–71, 72, 81, 127
Brethren of the Common Life, 28, 33, 68, 84, 128
Brothers of the Christian Schools, 86
Brothers of St John of God, 87
Camaldolese, 27, 29
Canons of Windesheim, 28, 33, 63
Capuchins, 14, 27, 38, 72, 114
Carmelites, 64–5, 69, 72
Carthusians, 18, 27–8, 33, 34, 41, 57, 73
Cistercians, 81
Clerks regular Ministers of the Sick, 87
Clerks regular of the Pious Schools, 85
Dominicans, 17, 27, 62–3, 69, 72, 81
Franciscans, 33, 34, 57, 80; observant, 27
Friars minims, 69
Jesuates, 87
Jesuits, 14, 38–9, 41–2, 99; St Ignatius, the *Spiritual Exercises*, and, 43–66 *passim*, 126–32; and the religious life, 73–80; authority and obedience in, 80–3, 130; and education, 78–9, 84, 114; and missions, 122, 137, 141–2; 'presbyterianism' of, 136; Dutch, 141; English, 131, 141
Oratorians, 13, 17, 41, 84
Oratory of Divine Love, 13, 26, 87
Servites, 69, 71
Somaschi, 17, 74
Theatines, 17, 18, 26, 40, 74, 77, 114
religious orders, etc., of women:
  women and the religious life, 19, 84–5, 144
  Benedictines, 39–40
  Carmelites, 39, 64–5
  Institute of Mary, 85, 144
  Sisters of Charity, 85
  Ursulines, 84, 85
Richelieu, Armand du Plessis de, cardinal, 141
Rigault, Georges, 86
Ritter, M., 6
Rode, Johann de, 34
Rupp, Gordon, 31
Ruysbroeck, Jan van, 34, 64

sacraments: Counter-Reformation and frequentation of, 37, 140; communion, 37–40, 140; confession, 37; confirmation, 136 n.; holy orders, 136

# Index